SCORE READING,
FORM AND HISTORY

SCORE READING, FORM AND HISTORY

A Graded Music Course for Schools, Book IV

ANNIE O. WARBURTON
MUS.D., L.R.A.M., A.R.C.M.

LONGMAN

LONGMAN GROUP LIMITED
London

*Associated companies, branches and representatives
throughout the world*

© Annie O. Warburton 1959

First published 1959
Ninth impression 1970

ISBN 0 582 32589 7

Cover design based on part of the original
score of *Armide* by Gluck

*Printed in Hong Kong by
Dai Nippon Printing Co (International) Ltd*

ACKNOWLEDGEMENTS

We are indebted to Messrs Augener Ltd for an extract from Corelli: 'Allémanda' from Sonata, Op. 4, No. 2, revised by Joachim & Chrysander, and Messrs Boosey & Hawkes Ltd for extracts from Handel: 'Concerto Grosso No. 12': Largo; Mozart: 'Symphony in G minor', K.550; Haydn: 'Emperor Quartet', Op. 76, No. 3; Beethoven: 'Symphony No. 2 in D'; Weber: 'Overture to Der Freischütz'; Tschaikowsky: 'Casse Noisette' Suite; and Britten: 'Young Person's Guide'.

NOTE TO THE TEACHER

This book is primarily intended for the upper forms in grammar schools; but it may also prove useful for students in training colleges, and, indeed, for music students of all kinds.

Though following on from the first three books of *A Graded Music Course*, it is complete in itself, and can be used quite independently, if desired. It presupposes that the student has sufficient knowledge of music to be able to follow music quotations, and to understand such terms as "modulation to the dominant".

It is so planned that it may be used by classes which are not specialising in music, in any part of the upper school, as, for example, fifth- or sixth-form "appreciation" classes; or by music candidates for the O level G.C.E., who should find it gives them the background they need for the study of their prescribed works. Together with the author's *Harmony* and *Melody Writing and Analysis* it completes the course for such candidates.

With either type of class the author believes that the teacher should have freedom to choose his examples for himself. In the case of a general "appreciation" class they may be linked with concert-going or radio-listening, or may depend upon the records the school happens to have available; while the G.C.E. class will have certain prescribed works to study each year, and may have little time to give to any others. Accordingly the information given here is so planned that it can be applied to any examples the teacher wishes. Some G.C.E. teachers spend a considerable part of their lesson time in dictating notes. This book provides the required information, thus leaving the teacher free to devote much more time to the actual hearing of music.

The serious study of large-scale musical works, whether

for examination purposes or for recreative enjoyment, requires a knowledge of musical instruments and score reading, the elements of musical form, and a background of musical history. Few schools can afford a book on each of these subjects for each individual pupil, nor is it easy to find books which give just the right amount of information for this stage. For example, books on instruments tend to be either too simple, giving information about the sound and appearance of the instruments but little about their notation or about score reading; or too difficult, being intended for the musician who wishes to write for an orchestra. In all three parts of this book the author has tried to give the amount of information suited to the student at this stage.

The first part of the book deals with instruments from the point of view of the student who wishes to follow a score. The subject is treated historically, and quotations are given from a number of scores of gradually increasing complexity. They have been chosen from works that many schools will already have in their library, in the hope that, having studied one page in detail, the class may then go on to hear the complete work while following the score. But it will be equally good to follow the score of some other similar work which is available, or which is required for examination purposes. A G.C.E. class whose only prescribed orchestral score is one by Haydn will find all that is necessary in Chapters One to Three, and, if time is short, may omit the rest of this section. Drawings of the more important obsolete instruments and photographs of the chief present-day ones are included.

The second part of the book summarises the chief musical forms. Again, the approach is largely historical, which means that it can easily be linked with the other two sections of the book, and applied to whatever works are desired. For example, fugue may be omitted by G.C.E. candidates who do not require it for their prescribed works. The teacher who is not tied by particular examination requirements may be glad to make use of the suggested examples of each type of form. The essential thing is that examples should always be heard.

The final part of the book gives an outline of musical history. No musical work can be fully appreciated until it is placed into its appropriate background. The essential musical developments are traced here, so that the growth of music is shown as a continuous whole.

At the end of Chapters Fourteen to Nineteen there are brief biographies of the chief composers mentioned in the chapter, together with a list of their more important works. These aim at providing sufficient background information about the composers most likely to be required for examination purposes, together with the dates that some of these examinations demand. But wherever possible, it should be supplemented by general reading from a well-stocked music library. Composers such as Liszt, Verdi, Franck, Grieg and Rimsky-Korsakov are not included in these biographies, though they are referred to in the main text, because, for differing reasons, their works are not likely to be set for G.C.E. O Level, or similar examinations. And only those modern composers whose works are frequently prescribed are included, though, again, there is reference to others in the main text. If the work of a lesser composer, such as Humperdinck, happens to be set, the student will have to make use of other books, or be provided with notes by the teacher. Considerations of space make it impossible to include biographies of every composer of note, so examination requirements appear to be the best criterion.

These biographies are in note form and in smaller print because they are not an essential part of the text; and any that are not required for a particular purpose can be omitted without affecting the historical continuity.

It must be realised that the facts and information given in this book are valueless until they are brought to life by musical illustrations. The book should be a useful adjunct to teaching, but it is not meant to take the place of the teacher; and it is upon the teacher that the musical value of the course depends.

CONTENTS

PHOTOGRAPHS

The photographs are reproduced by permission of the B.B.C.

FOREIGN TERMS FOUND IN
ORCHESTRAL SCORES

English	Italian	German	French
Piccolo	Flauto piccolo	Kleine Flöte	Petite flûte
Flute	Flauto	Flöte	Flûte
Oboe	Oboe	Hoboe	Hautbois
Cor anglais	Corno Inglese	Englisch Horn	Cor anglais
Clarinet	Clarinetto	Klarinette	Clarinette
Bass clarinet	Clarinetto basso	Bass Klarinette	Clarinette basse
Bassoon	Fagotto	Fagott	Basson
Double bassoon	Contrafagotto	Kontrafagott	Contrebasson
Horn	Corno	Horn	Cor
Trumpet	Tromba	Trompete	Trompette
Trombone	Trombone	Posaune	Trombone
Tuba	Tuba	Tuba	Tuba
Timpani	Timpani	Pauken	Timbales
Bass drum	Gran cassa	Grosse Trommel	Grosse caisse
Side drum	Tamburo militaire	Kleine Trommel	Tambour militaire
Cymbals	Piatti	Becken	Cymbales
Tambourine	Tamburino	Tamburin	Tambour de Basque
Triangle	Triangolo	Triangel	Triangle
Tubular bells	Campanelle	Glocken	Cloches
Glockenspiel	Campanette	Glockenspiel	Jeu de timbres
Celesta	Celesta	Celesta	Celesta
Xylophone	Zilafone	Xylophon	Xylophone
Harp	Arpa	Harfe	Harpe
Violin	Violino	Violine	Violon
Viola	Viola	Bratsche	Alto
'Cello	Violoncello	Violoncell	Violoncelle
Double bass	Contrabasso	Kontrabass	Contrebasse
Major	Maggiore	Dur	Majeur
Minor	Minore	Moll	Mineur
A	La	A	La
B	Si	H	Si
C	Do	C	Ut
D	Re	D	Re
E	Mi	E	Mi
F	Fa	F	Fa
G	Sol	G	Sol
Sharp	Diesis	"is" is added to letter. Eg. C♯ = Cis	Dièse
Flat	Bemolle	"es" is added to letter. Eg. C♭ = Ces, except B♭, which is called "B".	Bémol

PART ONE

MUSICAL INSTRUMENTS AND SCORE READING

Chapter One

The Earliest String Instruments

Man has fashioned musical instruments from the earliest times. In Europe they can be traced back for 25,000 years. The twang of the bow as the arrow left the string probably gave primitive man the first idea of making a string instrument. At first it did not occur to him to fit several strings to his bow and thus to make a harp; but archaeologists, exploring in the Middle East, have discovered pictures of harps and lutes dating as far back as 3000 B.C. Each country and each civilisation had its own variety of musical instruments. At first they were chiefly used for ritual purposes, but gradually the usage was extended to secular activities. We know that lyres were used in classical Greece (500–400 B.C.) to accompany poetry in the annual competitions during the Delphic Games, and that a similar instrument was used by the Celts in the first century B.C., to accompany their songs.

The Chest of Viols

Harps, lutes, lyres and other similar instruments were plucked. It is probable that bowed string instruments were first used in the East, and brought to Europe in the Middle Ages by Islam. By the time of Queen Elizabeth I a complete family of bowed string instruments was established. This was the "consort" of viols, and it usually consisted of four sizes: treble, alto, tenor and bass or viola da gamba. There

1

was also a double bass viol or violone. A set of viols was often kept in a chest, and provided the means by which a family could entertain itself. These instruments can be seen in museums today, and even heard, occasionally, in concerts of Elizabethan music. They all had six strings, and the fingerboard was fretted, like that of a guitar or banjo today. They were held downwards like a 'cello, and the bow was held sideways like a saw, instead of from above like a violin bow. Fantasies for viols by Weelkes and Byrd are available on gramophone records.

VIOL

The Violin Family

Another family of string instruments, the violin family, developed side by side with the viol family, and eventually superseded it. The first violins were made in the sixteenth century. Three famous Italian families, Amati, Guarneri and Stradivari, perfected the instrument in the seventeenth century. Instruments made by them are worth hundreds and even thousands of pounds today.

The members of the violin family are the violin, viola, violoncello ('cello) and double bass. They all have four strings, tuned thus:

(sounds an 8ve
lower)

In large orchestras one of the double basses may be a five-string "sub-contrabass". The extra string gives low C, a third lower than the bottom string shown above, and an octave below the lowest note of the 'cello. The 'cello uses the tenor clef for its higher notes; and occasionally the treble clef is used for the exceptionally high notes played by soloists.

The violin family is much more agile and expressive than the viol family, partly owing to the lack of frets, partly because each instrument has only four strings, and partly owing to the different shape and method of holding the bow; so the viol family died out in the eighteenth century.

All the instruments of the violin family can play a complete scale in their "first position", starting from the lowest string, and going up to a fourth or fifth above the top "open" string. By moving the hand along the fingerboard, further "positions" can be obtained, and it is comparatively easy to play an octave above the top string. Solo violinists and 'cellists often play considerably higher than this.

Bowing

A down bow is rather stronger than an up bow, and is therefore frequently used on a strong beat. ⊓ indicates a down bow, and ∨ an up bow, though these marks are rarely shown except in beginners' music. A separate movement of the bow can be made for each note. If more than one note is intended to be played with one bow this is shown by a slur over the notes concerned.   Various effects of phrasing, and of staccato and legato can be obtained by means of the bowing.

Sul ponticello means "play with the bow closer to the bridge than usual".   If playing loudly, this is harsh; if softly, it sounds weird and mysterious.

Sul tasto, or *sur la touche*, means "play with the bow closer to the finger board than usual".   This produces a soft, whispering tone.

Col legno is occasionally seen, and is an indication that the strings are to be played with the back of the bow (the wood), instead of with the hair.   It is used most effectively for the clattering of skeletons in Saint Saëns's 'Danse Macabre', and in the 'Mars' movement from Holst's 'The Planets'.

Other Effects

Pizzicato means that the strings are plucked with the finger.
Arco is an indication that the bow is to be used again.

Double stopping.   If two notes are played together the effect is known as "double stopping".   Chords of three and four notes are sometimes seen, but these have to be played in a quick arpeggio, as the bow cannot lie flat on more than two strings at once.

Harmonics are indicated by an "o" over the note.   The finger is placed lightly, instead of firmly on the string, at a place where one of the notes of the harmonic series occurs. Bowing then produces an ethereal effect.   (Further information about harmonics is given on p. 19.)

Mutes can be placed on the bridge to deaden the effect. They are rarely used on the double bass.   The effect is marked "con sordino"; and "senza sordino" shows a return to normal.

Division of Parts

In orchestras there is always more than one player to each string part.   The earliest orchestras were content with a few to each part; but a large modern orchestra may have as many as 16 first violins, 14 second violins, 12 violas, 10 'cellos and 8 double basses. Normally first violins, second violins, violas and 'cellos make four-part harmony together, with the basses strengthening the bass line by playing the 'cello part an octave lower; but many other arrangements are possible. A very rich effect is produced when all the strings play in unison and octaves; and sometimes composers divide the strings into eight or even more parts. In such cases the composer may write each part on a separate stave, but it is more common to write "divisi" over two notes on one stave. The first player at each desk then plays the top note, and the second player the bottom one. "Unis" indicates a return to the normal. "À 2", "à 3", and even "à 4" show a similar division of parts.

Keyboard Instruments. The Organ

Organs, in which the sound is produced by wind blowing through a series of pipes, were the first instruments to be played by means of a keyboard. There was a famous one in Winchester in the tenth century, but the mechanism was so heavy that considerable force had to be used to play the keys. Organs of various sizes were used throughout the Middle Ages. The organ pedals (a keyboard played by the feet) were invented in Germany in the fifteenth century. By Bach's time the organ, though clumsier than that of today, and operated by blowers instead of by electricity, was very similar to the present-day instrument, and was capable of being used for the finest music.

The Clavier or Klavier

This is a German word meaning "keyboard instrument". Although it is sometimes used for the keyboard of an organ, it is more usual to apply it to keyboard instruments in which the sound is produced by strings, such as clavichords, harpsichords and pianos. It should not be confused with "clavichord".

The Clavichord

This keyboard instrument was in use from the fifteenth to the eighteenth century. When the key was struck, a metal tangent rose and pressed the string. The tone was so soft that the instrument was useless except in a small room, but it could be varied to a certain extent, and we know that Bach was fond of the instrument. In shape it was like a rectangular box. It had no pedals, and its range varied from three to five octaves.

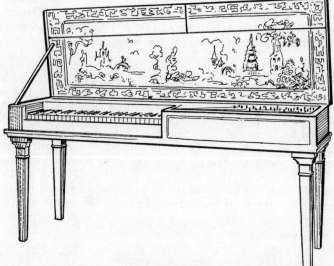

CLAVICHORD

The Spinet, Virginal and Harpsichord

The fundamental mechanism of these three instruments was the same. When the key was struck a quill plucked the strings. This produced a larger, brighter tone than that of the clavichord, but it could hardly be varied at all.

The virginal was popular in the sixteenth and seventeenth centuries, and was the same shape as the clavichord, and had the same range.   Queen Elizabeth I and Mary Queen of Scots were both accomplished players of the virginal.

The spinet was in use in the seventeenth and eighteenth centuries, and was wing shaped, thus looking rather like a small grand piano.   But it still had a small range and no pedals.

The harpsichord was the most highly developed of these instruments, and was used from the sixteenth to the eighteenth century.   Unlike the virginal or spinet, it had two or more strings to each note; and it looked quite like a grand piano.   Stops, like those of an organ, or pedals made it possible to vary the number of strings used for each note,

HARPSICHORD

and one string was often an octave higher or lower than the others.   A "swell" effect was also possible.   More elaborate harpsichords had two or even three keyboards; and, by varying the keyboards and the number of strings used, it was possible to get variations of strength and of tone colour.   But variations of finger pressure had little or no effect, and it was therefore difficult to accentuate a particular note, to produce gradual variations of volume, or to sustain tone.   This partly accounts for the large amount of ornamentation found in the Clavier music of seventeenth and eighteenth-century composers, such as Purcell, Bach and

Handel. As a note could not be emphasised by striking it more strongly, the accent was indicated by decorating it.

The harpsichord, being the largest and loudest of these early keyboard instruments, was always used for public performances, and those involving the use of other instruments or of choirs or orchestras.

Many of these early keyboard instruments were beautifully painted or inlaid, and even, sometimes, ornamented with precious stones. Occasionally the "white" keys were black and the "black" white.

Equal Temperament

F♯ and G♭ are not exactly the same sound when both are perfectly in tune. But whereas a string player can move his finger slightly to change the pitch, a clavier player has only one key to do duty for both. So it has to be tuned or "tempered".

Up to Bach's time it was *unequally* tempered. For example, the note between F and G was perfectly in tune for F♯, but out of tune for G♭. Similarly, the note between A and B was in tune for B♭ but not for A♯. The chromatic scale did not therefore consist of twelve equal semitones, and this meant that keys with many sharps and flats were badly out of tune and could not be used.

Bach objected to composers being hampered in this way, and he therefore tuned his Claviers to *equal* temperament, that is, with twelve equal semitones to the octave. This meant that the note between F and G was not exactly F♯ or G♭, but it was near enough to both not to sound unpleasant as either. To foster the growth of equal temperament he wrote twenty-four preludes and fugues, one in each major and minor key. Twenty years later he wrote another twenty-four, and these, taken together, are known as the 'Well-tempered Clavier', or, more popularly, as 'The 48'.

Continuo

With the beginnings of opera in the seventeenth century and the development of a harmonic style of writing, it became the custom for the composer to indicate his chords by means of figures written under a bass part, rather than write out each chord in detail. This "continuo" part was played as a single bass line by the 'cellos and basses, while the harpsichordist or the organist played it at the same time, but also filling in upper parts according to the figuring, arranged as he pleased. This continuo part was always present in chamber and orchestral and accompanied vocal music in the time of Bach and Handel, and one of the main differences between their music and that of Haydn and Mozart was that the latter ceased to write a continuo part. The continuo player obviously had to be very capable, in order to play from "figured bass" at sight. He was the most important person in the seventeenth- and eighteenth-century orchestra, and directed the performance from his instrument, as there was no conductor in those days.

The Piano

The pianoforte, or fortepiano, so called because it could be played both "soft" and "loud", was invented by Cristofori in Florence in 1709. The strings were struck by hammers, instead of by the tangent of the clavichord or the quill of the harpsichord, and the intention was to combine the tone gradation of the clavichord with the greater volume of the harpsichord. The instrument also possessed dampers, which silenced the strings when the fingers left the keys, as they do today. J. S. Bach heard some early German pianos and was critical at first, though he approved of later models. But he never possessed one.

Pianos, harpsichords and clavichords continued side by side in the second half of the eighteenth century. Haydn's and Mozart's "Clavier" sonatas were probably played on harpsichords more often than on pianos. Even Beethoven's early sonatas must often have been played on the harpsichord. But in his lifetime the English firm of Broadwood invented the sustaining pedal, and nineteenth- and twentieth-century piano music would be unthinkable without it—it has been called "the soul of the piano". The compass of the piano has also been increased gradually from 4 to $7\frac{1}{4}$ octaves.

It was natural that as piano action improved and pianos became more common on the concert platform and in the home, the harpsichord and clavichord should have died out. But the making of them has been revived recently, principally so that the works written in the eighteenth century and earlier can be played on the instruments for which they were written.

Score Reading

Following the music with the printed "score" is a great aid to both understanding and enjoyment, and often helps to increase one's concentration on the music. A single line of music is easy to follow, and most people with any knowledge of music notation can follow the two staves of a piano composition. But every extra stave adds to the difficulty. It is helpful to practise orchestral score reading in stages, dealing with its growth historically, so that proficiency and enjoyment are gained in this useful skill.

Corelli's Sonatas

Corelli (1653–1713) was the first great violin composer, performer and teacher. He wrote many sonatas for two violins with a continuo part to be played by the 'cello as a single line and by the harpsichord or organ in harmony. The original score consisted of three melodic lines, with figuring under the bass, but modern editors usually arrange the continuo part for the piano as shown below. The 'cello plays the bass line of the piano part.

If there are violinists and 'cellists in your class you may be able to arrange a performance of this short extract, while the rest of you follow the score. It should be played two or three times, so that you are able to follow each part in turn. The school library may contain a set of copies of a similar work, which you can follow while listening to a performance, perhaps on records.

Purcell and other contemporaries wrote in a similar style.

CORELLI : SONATA II, OP. 4

(Augener p. 9).

ALLEMANDA

The Concerto Grosso

Orchestral music by Corelli, Bach and Handel usually consisted of solo parts played by the more accomplished instrumentalists, called the "concertante" or "concertino", and the main body of strings, called the "ripieno". If everyone played together it was called a "tutti". A harpsichord or organ played a continuo part throughout the ripieno sections. The "concerto grosso", as this type of work was called, was the forerunner of the symphony, rather than the concerto, of a later period. The concertante might consist of any combination of string, woodwind or brass instruments, often depending upon what the composer had available for the particular performance he had in mind.

Bach's six Brandenburg concertos are concerti grossi. The concertante of no. 1 consists of two horns, three oboes, bassoon and violino piccolo (a small violin); of no. 2, flute, oboe, trumpet and violin; of no. 4, two flutes and a violin; of no. 5, flute, violin and harpsichord. Nos. 3 and 6 have no specific concertante; but no. 3 is for strings divided into 10 contrapuntal voices to provide contrasts between the various possible groupings of the instruments; while no. 6, which is also for strings, but without violins, uses two of the violas and a bass as a contrasting group.

Both Corelli and Handel wrote twelve concerti grossi for strings. Here is a short complete movement from Handel's twelfth concerto grosso. Try to play the ripieno on the piano, and then add the concertante parts by playing or singing them, if possible. Remember that the harpsichord would be playing a continuo part, based on the figuring shown above, at the same time.

Take the opportunity, if possible, of following the performance of some orchestral work of this period with the score.

Chamber Music

Chamber music is music for a small room, in contrast to music for a church, theatre or concert hall. In the seven-

HANDEL : CONCERTO GROSSO, NO. 12

(Boosey and Hawkes score, p. 22)

teenth and eighteenth centuries the term included vocal and solo works; but nowadays it is usually confined to solo instrumentalists performing in combination, though the term "chamber orchestra" is sometimes applied to a small orchestra of chamber proportions. Chamber music has been written for very many combinations of soloists; but the most common, and the combination with the most literature, is the string quartet.

The String Quartet

Haydn and Mozart were the first great writers of the string quartet, and the first ones to cease writing a continuo part in their chamber and orchestral music.

Haydn's early quartets are easy to follow from score, as the first violin has the tune most of the time, with the second violin, viola and 'cello playing harmonic accompaniments. But in his later quartets he gave the lower instruments more interesting contrapuntal parts, and this makes them rather harder for you to follow, both visually and aurally. But they are more interesting for the performers, and have much more to offer the listener, once he learns how to follow the different parts, and to realise their relative importance at any given moment.

The quotation given here is from Haydn's 'Emperor' quartet, op. 76, no. 3, and it is chosen because so many schools have scores and records of this work. The third variation of the slow movement is easy to read because the viola part, which you normally find the hardest to follow on account of the unfamiliar clef, consists of the theme, which you know. Try playing the viola and 'cello parts on the piano, while someone else plays or sings the violin parts.

Now follow any string quartet score that you happen to have available, while listening to the music.

HAYDN: 'EMPEROR' QUARTET, OP. 76, NO. 3
(Boosey and Hawkes score, p. 14)

Chapter Two

The **Double Reed** Instruments. The **Oboe** and **Bassoon**

The oboe, cor anglais, bassoon and double bassoon are all members of the same family. This family has been in regular orchestral use longer than any other woodwind family. Its ancestors were the shawms and pommers of the Middle Ages. Shawms were made in seven sizes. At a later stage they were called "hautbois", and Louis XIV had an orchestra of them. Pommers or bombards were the ancestors of the bassoon. The gross bass pommer was ten feet long and had to be supported by someone else's shoulder or by a trestle in church!

When Bach and Handel wrote for an orchestra which included wind instruments, the oboes and bassoons were the chief instruments used. They often doubled the string parts, and in a vocal work they might double the voice parts. Sometimes quite large numbers were employed. The early instruments had no keys to cover the holes, and if the fingers left a slight gap, a squeak would result!

The modern oboes and bassoons date from the time of Haydn and Mozart. Improvements in mechanism and tone have been made since, but in essentials the instruments are unchanged. Most orchestral works of this period had parts for oboes and bassoons, usually two of each. Flutes were not always present, and clarinets only began to be used at the end of the period. So oboes and bassoons were the mainstay of the woodwind.

The oboe. The range of the modern oboe is

though the extreme notes are rarely used. It has a conical bore; and by pressing down a "speaker key" and blowing slightly differently, notes can be produced an octave higher with the same fingering—that is, it "overblows" at the octave, like the recorder. It is held downwards. Two reeds, fastened together, are inserted in the mouthpiece, and vibrate against each other when the player inserts them in his mouth and blows through them. The tone is very "reedy" and nasal: plaintive and pastoral when played slowly, playful or spiteful when played quickly. The oboe is the wind instrument least capable of variation of tuning, so it sets the standard and gives the "A" from which the orchestra takes its pitch.

Handel wrote two oboe concertos. Mozart wrote a quartet for oboe and strings, and there are many famous passages in orchestral works where the oboe can be heard to advantage, such as the opening of the slow movements of Schubert's "Great" C major symphony and Brahms's violin concerto, and the beginning of Tschaikowsky's 'Swan Lake' suite. Quick passages are heard in the scherzo of Beethoven's 'Pastoral' symphony; and the oboe represents the duck in Prokofiev's 'Peter and the Wolf'.

The bassoon. The range of the modern bassoon is

from which it will be seen that the tenor clef is used for the higher notes, as for the higher notes of the 'cello, in order to avoid leger lines. The top D, E and F are rarely used in orchestral music. Like the oboe, it has a conical bore, overblows at the octave, has a double reed and a nasal, plaintive tone. Like the oboe too, it can be used for slow, expressive melodies or for humorous staccato passages.

Unlike the upper woodwind instruments, it rarely plays a long solo, though if you get the opportunity of listening to Mozart's bassoon concerto you will hear it in all its moods.

2

If you listen to the waltz in Tschaikowsky's fifth symphony in E minor you will hear the bassoon play the second stanza of the main theme in octaves with the oboe, 19 bars from the beginning. Then 10 bars later, at the return to the first part of the theme, it plays in unison with the clarinet. 12 bars later again, you will hear it in an 8-bar solo, accompanied only by pizzicato strings. The bassoon often doubles the violin or some upper woodwind instrument in this way. Other well-known instances of its use are in 'L'Apprenti Sorcier' by Dukas, where it represents the broomstick, and in Prokofiev's 'Peter and the Wolf', where it represents the grandfather.

The Recorder and Flute

This family of woodwind instruments has no reed at all, and the tone is therefore soft and pure. Its origins go far back into antiquity. There are two types: those blown from the end, such as the recorder, and those blown through a hole in the side, such as the modern flute.

The Recorder. Recorders were very popular in the Tudor period. They were made in many sizes, and households used to own a chest of recorders, just as they had a chest of viols. The French type of instrument, called the flageolet, became popular in England a little later, and Pepys often speaks of playing it in his diary. The upper portion contained a sponge, to catch the moisture! Bach and Handel's flute parts were mostly written for the end-blown recorder type of flute, known as the "flûte à bec". However, when, in 1717, Bach heard the transverse flute, the kind blown sideways, he began to write for it; and for a short time, parts for both kinds of flutes existed side by side. Eventually the modern transverse flute became the main orchestral instrument and the recorder almost died out. But not quite! A few recorders still existed, and Arnold Dolmetsch and his family used to give concerts of old music with the old instruments.

One day, his old recorder was stolen from his luggage, so he
set to work to make a new one; and the modern use of
recorders in Britain dates from this event!   Now they are
particularly popular in schools, because they are not difficult
to play or expensive to buy, and their tone is very pleasant.
Unfortunately they are not powerful enough to play in a
modern symphony orchestra.

The Flute.   The flute now has keys to cover the holes, and
the modern mechanism makes it easier to play than in Bach's
day, but, on the whole, it has changed very little.   Its range
is

and it is very agile.   Like the oboe, it overblows at the octave.   Its lower notes are soft and rich, while its upper notes
are brilliant.   It often doubles the tune played by some other
instrument, such as the violin or oboe, an octave higher.
You cannot always hear it in such cases, but it brightens the
tone of the main instrument.

Mozart's quartet for flute and strings is a good illustration
of flute tone.   Mendelssohn's scherzo from 'A Midsummer
Night's Dream' expects the flautist to play 240 semiquavers
non-stop at the end of the piece!   Another famous example
of flute tone is in the 'Dance of the Little Flutes' from
Tschaikowsky's 'Nutcracker' suite.

Haydn and Mozart usually wrote for one or two flutes in
their symphonies, and since their time two flutes are always
required in an orchestra.

The Harmonic Series

Before you can understand the mechanism and notation of
brass instruments you must know something about the
harmonic series.   Imagine a string or a column of air which,
when made to vibrate, produces the sound

By halving the string or making the column of air vibrate

in halves you will get the sound an octave higher. Divisions of a third will produce the sound a fifth above again, and similar higher ratios produce the following, known as the "harmonic series".

The lowest note is known as the "fundamental" sound, and the rest are called "harmonics", "upper partials" or "overtones". Theoretically the series goes on to infinity.

A tuning fork, when struck, produces only its fundamental note. But a note played on any kind of musical instrument produces harmonics of greater or less strength, in addition to the fundamental sound of which you are conscious, varying from the recorder which produces nearly a "pure" note to church bells in which harmonics are strongly present. The only reason for contrasts in tone colour between, for example, the violin, flute, clarinet or trumpet sounding the same note with equal strength, lies in the differing number and intensity of different harmonics present with the fundamental sound. For example, the clarinet sounds hollow because the even-numbered harmonics are left out completely, the trumpet is bright because the high overtones are relatively strong.

So far we have considered sounds in which the fundamental note is coloured by the presence of overtones which are not consciously heard. But one can blow a wind instrument in such a way that one of the overtones becomes the main sound, because the column of air is vibrating, for example, in halves, thus producing the sound an octave higher. The shape of the tube and the type of mouthpiece affect what can be done in this way.

Bugle players can only produce the notes of the harmonic series from 3 to 6—you will realise you can play "Come to the cookhouse door, boys" on these four sounds. Horn

players can play from the fundamental sound to about
number 12; while trumpeters in Bach's day produced the
higher rather than the lower notes of the series, in order to
get a complete scale.

A simple instrument like the bugle has no other means of
producing different sounds. Horns and trumpets used to
have crooks and now they have valves; while trombones
have a slide. All these devices are used to produce more
notes by changing to a different harmonic series.

The Horn

The "natural" horn, which was in orchestral use until
the end of the nineteenth century, was able to play the notes
2 to 12 of one harmonic series, mainly by means of varying

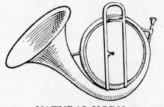

NATURAL HORN

lip pressure. The player had to be allowed time to insert
an extra piece of tubing, called a "crook" if he wished to
make the vibrating column of air longer and thus get a
lower harmonic series. This meant, for example, that a
horn player could play the opening theme of Beethoven's
'Eroica' symphony

by crooking his instrument in the key of E♭, but he could not
play a complete scale in *any* key.

It was the custom for the horn parts always to be written
in the key of C, which means that in music written before
the middle of the nineteenth century you will normally only

see notes 2 to 12 of the harmonic series shown above. But occasionally a composer wanted another note so badly that he asked the performer to fake it by putting his hand in the bell. Such "stopped" notes were never very satisfactory, however. They were shown thus " + ".

But this did not mean that the horn could only *play* in the key of C. The composer wrote "Horn in F" or "Horn in G" at the beginning, which meant that the player used his crook for that key, and produced a harmonic series a fifth or fourth lower than what was written. It was easy for the player because, having put in his crook, he could forget about the actual pitch, and always blow in the same way for the same harmonic. But it means that the conductor and score reader have to transpose the part from the key of C down to the key in which the instrument is crooked, in order to know what he is actually playing.

The easiest way for you to read a natural horn part is to think in sol-fa. Look at the horn part in the minuet of Mozart's G minor symphony quoted on p. 25. The first notes are *written* as doh¹ soh in the key of C. But they *sound* doh¹ soh in the key of G. Play the horn parts in this quotation on the piano as they actually sound. Remember that the crooks make the column of air *longer*, so the part always sounds *lower* than it looks. A horn crooked in C actually sounds an octave lower. Except when using the first few notes of the harmonic series, which are rare, the horn part is written on the treble staff, but owing to the downward transposition the range corresponds roughly to that of alto and tenor voices.

It was the custom in Haydn and Mozart's day to use two horns. But they were not always crooked in the same key. In the first movement of the symphony whose minuet is quoted on p. 25, Mozart uses one crooked in B♭ and the other crooked in G, so as to have more notes of the key of G minor available. You will realise that he could not get the complete tonic triad of G minor with either crook. Also, when he comes to his second subject in the relative major, B♭, his B♭ crook comes in useful. If a composer changes his crook during a movement, he writes "muta F in E♭", and has to allow some time for the performer to make the change. Mozart changes crooks 35 times in the opera 'Don Giovanni'.

There is a famous horn passage at the beginning of Weber's overture 'Der Freischütz', in which he uses four horns, two in F and two in C, so as to have more notes available. And during the nineteenth century it became quite common to use four horns for this reason. With the invention of valves, which will be discussed in Chapter Four, it might have been possible to have gone back to two, but by then four had become general. Some composers even occasionally use six or eight.

Horn players train their lips to play either the higher or the lower notes of the harmonic series. If there are four horns in an orchestra the first and third players play the high notes, and the second and fourth the low ones. The first and second horn parts are usually written on one stave and the third and fourth on another.

The horn is one of the most difficult orchestral instruments to play, and even in the best orchestras one occasionally hears a "muffed" note. But it has a beautiful, warm, poetic tone, and in addition to playing solos quite frequently in modern works, it is used most of the time to hold the texture together, so to speak, often playing repeated or long holding notes in the middle register between the melody in the higher string or wind instruments, and the instruments supplying the bass. The nocturne from Mendelssohn's 'A Midsummer Night's Dream' provides a beautiful example of horns playing quietly, as does also the *andante* from Tschaikowsky's fifth symphony. But, when played loudly, the horn can sound almost like a trumpet, as in Siegfried's horn call by Wagner, or in 'Till Eulenspiegel' by Strauss.

The Position of the Instruments in a Full Score

Nowadays it is the custom to place all the woodwind instruments at the top of the score, and these are followed by the brass. The horns and trumpets are written in C major, so a quick glance, to see which staves have no key signature, helps to place them. Percussion parts follow, and the strings come together at the bottom of the score.   The string parts are the most important, and they play as a group most of the time, so it is obviously an advantage to keep them together.   The 'cellos and the basses must be at the bottom of the score, as they play the bass part more continuously than any other instruments.   This grouping means that the first violin part is rather difficult to find, yet the person new to score reading is advised to follow it most of the time, as it has the tune more often than any other part.   Some editions separate the strings from the parts above in some way, or bracket the first and second violin parts together, as an aid to finding their position.

Practise turning over the pages of a score and seeing how quickly you can find the violin part on each page.   In the early stages of score reading while listening to the gramophone, it may be a help if your teacher calls out "turn", or "page 28", as an indication of where your eye should be. When you get more experienced your eye will be able to leap from the violin part to that of some other instrument when your ear tells you it has an important part.   If you can hear the same movement several times with a score, try following a different instrument or group of instruments each time.

The Symphonies of Haydn and Mozart

Haydn is often called the "father of the symphony".   He established the general lay-out of the symphony orchestra, and the harpsichord continuo part died out.   The strings were the mainstay of the orchestra.   For woodwind he used two oboes and two bassoons, and often one or two flutes.   In his later works, after the clarinet came into use, he began to use two clarinets also.   Mozart also used clarinets in a few of his last symphonies.   But many Haydn and Mozart symphonies are without clarinet parts.   In the brass section both composers used two horns and two trumpets, and for percussion they used timpani.   But the trumpets and timpani usually did little more than mark the cadences and provide excitement in the noisier passages, and they were often silent

MOZART: SYMPHONY IN G MINOR

(Boosey and Hawkes score, p. 40)

III

in the slow movements. So you can follow many Haydn and Mozart scores quite well without knowing about clarinets, trumpets and drums, which are left for the next chapter.

In Mozart's last three great symphonies, the one in E♭ has no oboes, the Jupiter has no clarinets, and the G minor was written without clarinets at first, though the composer added them later. This last symphony also has no trumpets or drums. Study the scoring of the first section of the minuet given on p. 25. There is a good deal of "doubling" of parts. Most of the time the flute plays an octave above the violin, thus brightening the tone. The second violins play in unison or in octaves with the firsts. The bassoons mostly double the 'cellos and basses, and the oboes, horns and violas provide inner harmonies. (The Boosey and Hawkes score gives the additional clarinet parts, but they can be ignored for the purposes of reading this page of score, as they play exactly the same notes as the oboes. They are not given in the Eulenberg score.) It may be helpful to play each part on the piano, and some of you might even make an attempt to put it all together, though it would be easier to try this as a duet. Four people at two pianos, one piano representing wind and the other the strings, should find it quite easy. But play the horn parts by themselves first.

Now follow as many Haydn and Mozart scores as you can, while listening to the gramophone. You can learn even more by taking the score to a concert, when both eye and ear can link the score with the performers. The more you practise score reading, the more details you will notice, and the more pleasure you will get from an orchestral work.

Chapter Three

The Clarinet

The clarinet family is the youngest of the woodwind families in the orchestra. It consists of instruments with a single reed which vibrates against the mouthpiece of the instrument.

It grew from a "chalumeau", a simple instrument never used in orchestras. The chalumeau had a restricted range which corresponded to the lowest notes of the modern clarinet, and these notes are still spoken of as being in the chalumeau register.

The clarinet was first used about 1700, and it was gradually improved during the century. But it took a surprisingly long time to get into regular orchestral use, and at first it was used merely to double or to replace the oboes.

Mozart heard the clarinet in the Mannheim orchestra in 1778 and wrote most enthusiastically about it to his father. The same year he used it in his 'Paris' symphony, and there is a delightful instance of its use in the trio of his E♭ symphony. He treated the instrument much more effectively than did Haydn. By the time of Beethoven it had become the custom to include two in the orchestra. The system of fingering and the intonation has been improved since then, but the range and tone quality of the instrument has remained the same.

The range of the clarinet is written as

The tube is cylindrical and is "stopped" at one end by the reed, and it cannot therefore "over-blow" the even-numbered harmonics. So the first harmonic it can make

use of is a twelfth above the bottom note. Compare this
with the flute and oboe which can repeat their lowest octave
an octave higher by overblowing, while using the same
fingering.

The lowest octave, the chalumeau register, is rich and
powerful; the next fifth is rather poor, owing to mechanical
difficulties. But when the twelfth from the bottom note is
reached and the notes can be overblown, the tone is good and
clear. There is a liquid quality throughout the whole range
which is peculiar to the clarinet, and it will be seen that its
range is much wider than that of any other upper woodwind
instrument. It is the most versatile of them all, and can
play as quickly as the flute and as melodiously as the oboe,
in addition to possessing its almost menacing low notes. It
has a wide range of dynamics, can play arpeggios well, and
is also very useful for accompaniment figures.

Mozart, Weber and Brahms were three exceptionally
good writers for the clarinet, and all were stimulated to
compose for it by some famous clarinet player. They all
three wrote a quintet for clarinet and strings, as well as other
chamber music works using the instrument, and Mozart and
Weber wrote concertos for it. There are many famous
instances of the orchestral use of the clarinet, such as the trio
from Mozart's E♭ symphony referred to above. The opening of Tschaikowsky's symphony in E minor provides a good
illustration of its chalumeau register, and the clarinet is
ideally suited to represent the cat in Prokofiev's 'Peter and
the Wolf'. It is much used in military bands, where
clarinets, in large numbers and in several sizes, take the place
of the violins in the orchestra. It is also very popular in
dance bands today.

Clarinets are transposing instruments. But the reason for
this is different from the reason given in the last chapter for
the horn. They *can* play any note within their range, but,
because of overblowing at the twelfth and the resultant
awkwardnesses of fingering, keys with a large number of
sharps and flats are difficult. They are avoided by making
clarinets in various sizes, which transpose up or down according to their size, and the composer chooses the size that will

give the player an easy key.   The player always connects the same finger position with the same note on the staff, but the sound is different according to the size of the instrument he is using.

There are two standard sizes in the symphony orchestra, the B♭ and the A, though you will occasionally find clarinet parts in C, which do not transpose.   (Look at the table of foreign names at the beginning of this book, and you will understand why "Klarinette in B" in German is the same as "clarinet in B♭" in English.)   The B♭ instrument is used for flat keys and the A for sharp keys.   If you write the scale of C, the B♭ instrument will sound the scale of B♭, a tone lower, and the A instrument will sound the scale of A, a minor third lower.   Therefore to make the B♭ instrument *sound* the scale of C you will have to write a tone *higher*, in D; and the part for the A instrument will have to be written a minor third higher, in E♭.

If you find this confusing, remember that the clarinet is really playing in the same key as the flute and oboe and other non-transposing instruments; and all you have to do is to transpose the clarinet part into the same key.   Here are two examples: a symphony in E♭ will use B♭ clarinets.   They will be written in F (an easy key) but sound in E♭, the key of the symphony.   A symphony in E will use A clarinets. They will be written in G (another easy key) but will again sound in the key of the symphony, E major.   Work out for yourself what keys would have to be used by the unfortunate player if the symphony in E♭ had used A clarinets and the symphony in E the B♭ instruments.

Look at the two extracts from Beethoven's symphony in D shown on pp. 34, 35.   The clarinets *sound* in the key of D, the key of the piece, but they are written in the key of F because clarinets in A are used and these are always written a minor third higher than they sound.   Play the clarinet parts on the piano in the key of D, their actual pitch.   You will see that, in the second extract, the clarinets have the tune for four bars, and that they are playing an octave higher than the bassoons.

Clarinets are made in other sizes too, but these are rarely

used in the symphony orchestra. The small clarinet in E♭ is much used in the military band. The bass clarinet will be referred to in the next chapter.

The Trumpet

This is another very old kind of instrument. It is mentioned in the bible and is known in every part of the world. Henry VIII had 42 instrumentalists attached to his court, and 14 of them played the trumpet!

The trumpet developed curves in the fifteenth century, but it was still confined to the notes of one harmonic series, a limitation which trumpet makers and trumpet performers tried to overcome in various ways in the next few hundred years. The trumpeters of Bach and Handel's day got a complete scale by blowing very hard so as to produce the upper notes of the harmonic series, but by the time of Haydn and Mozart they had reverted to lower notes again, and this is why trumpet parts of this period are largely confined to playing with the drums at the cadences and the climaxes; they could not play a complete scale and therefore never had a "tune".

NATURAL TRUMPET

Trumpet makers experimented with a slide mechanism like that of the trombone family, particularly in England, but it was not very successful. And Haydn wrote a concerto for an experimental trumpet with keys.

But the most common method of obtaining more notes, from Bach's time until the middle of last century, was to use extra crooks, similar to those used by the horn. In addition, a trumpeter often had several different-sized trumpets available, each one of which might have several crooks.

The trumpet, like the horn, was therefore a transposing instrument, and for the same reason. Its part was written in the key of C, and an indication of the instrument or crook required was shown at the beginning of the score. But there is one difference in the transposition of horn and trumpet parts. The horn always sounds lower than it is written, but the trumpet usually sounds higher. A trumpet part crooked in D or any note up to A♭ will sound higher than it is written, while a trumpet crooked in B♭ or A will sound lower and one in C does not transpose at all.

Look at the horn and trumpet parts in the two extracts from Beethoven's symphony in D given on pp. 34, 35. They are both crooked in D, and they apparently play the same notes. But the trumpets sound an octave higher than the horns. Play the horn and trumpet parts in both these extracts, at their actual pitch, on the piano.

Another point to notice is that horns are always written above the trumpets in the score, but trumpets are the higher sounding instruments. They are the treble of the brass group. Older trumpets used the same written harmonic series as the horn, but they tended to be crooked in higher keys. Modern valve trumpets use the harmonic series an octave higher, so they get the higher notes more easily.

Purcell's 'Trumpet Voluntary', Handel's 'Let the bright Seraphim' from 'Samson' and 'The Trumpet shall sound' from 'The Messiah', and the exciting trumpet part in Bach's 'Gloria in Excelsis' from the 'Mass in B minor' are all examples of early trumpet parts using the higher notes of the harmonic series. As explained above, trumpet parts of the earliest symphonies did little more than play the dominant and tonic at cadences. But with the invention of valves, which will be described in the next chapter, trumpet parts became much more exciting. Wagner made particularly good use of the valved trumpet, and you will have heard the wonderful things the modern trumpet can do in the dance band.

Modern trumpets and horns are sometimes muted by the insertion of a cone in the bell. You may have heard this effect, too, in the dance band. A mute changes the tone colour, and is used for both loud and soft passages. Muted brass represents a flock of sheep in Strauss's 'Don Quixote'.

The Timpani

The timpani are the only kind of drums which can produce a note of exact pitch, and they therefore find a place in every symphony orchestra.

They are Arabian in origin, and were brought to Europe by the Crusaders.   Calfskin is tightly stretched over a metal cauldron and is adjusted by six to eight taps round the edge. A half-turn on each tap raises the pitch by about a semitone. But this is never exact, and the intonation has to be checked by listening.   Mechanical tuners have been invented, but they are not popular in England, neither are they very reliable, as every skin is different, and rooms are subjected to changes of atmosphere which affect the pitch.

In early classical times it was the custom to use two timpani. The larger one had a range of and the smaller and they almost invariably played the tonic and dominant of the key.   Last century three became more general, and a few notes above and below the octave F to F are now occasionally written. The pitch of the timpani is changed quite often during the movement in modern works, but the player has to be given several bars' rest, in order to do this.

Timpani can play single notes, quick-time patterns or drum rolls, and different effects are produced today by using different kinds of drum sticks.   Trumpets and drums were generally used together in classical times to mark the cadences in tutti passages, and a crescendo drum roll could lead to a most effective climax.   But sometimes they had a more important part to play, as, for example, in the opening figure in Beethoven's violin concerto, which is frequently used throughout the movement.   Berlioz experimented a good deal with timpani, and was often most lavish in his use of them.

Reading a Score by Beethoven
and his Contemporaries

Haydn, in his later works, Beethoven, and the early romantics such as Mendelssohn, normally used an orchestra consisting of two flutes, two oboes, two clarinets, two bassoons, two horns, two trumpets, two timpani and strings. Trombones are sometimes found, and an occasional piccolo; and Berlioz, who was an early romantic composer, was much more ambitious and experimental. But most works of this period kept to this standard orchestra.

On pp. 34 and 35 are given the first page of the full score of Beethoven's symphony no. 2 in D, and a page showing the entry of the second subject in the first movement. Look down the names of the instruments, which are given in Italian, the most common language used in orchestral scores. Remember that "trombe" are trumpets, not trombones, and refer to the list of foreign names given at the beginning of this book. Notice that the second page has two scores to the page, and that instruments which are not required on these particular bars of score are omitted. You can easily tell the clarinet stave because it has a different signature; and horns, trumpets and drums stand out because they have none. The names of the instruments are given in an abbreviated form on this second page, and the keys of the clarinets, horns and trumpets are not shown. Study these two pages carefully and play each instrumental part on the piano.

The Trombone

Trombones were called sackbuts in the Middle Ages. Bach and Handel used them occasionally, but they mainly doubled the voice parts. Mozart used them in his opera 'The Magic Flute', but not in his symphonies. One of the earliest symphonies to use them was Beethoven's fifth, where they were introduced into the last movement. Schubert used them most effectively in his "Unfinished" and "Great"

3

(Boosey and Hawkes score, p. 1)

SYMPHONY № 2

L. van Beethoven, Op. 36
(1770-1827)

Flute

Clarinet and Bass Clarinet (left)

Bassoon and Double Bassoon (right)

Oboe

Trombone

(*Boosey and Hawkes score, p. 13*)

C major symphonies; and from then onwards they became an integral part of the symphony orchestra.

Trombones have always changed from one harmonic series to another by means of a slide. There are seven positions, each lowering the harmonic series by one semitone. As trombones have always had a complete scale available, they are not transposing instruments. They are made in several sizes. Beethoven used an alto trombone with the alto clef, a tenor with the tenor clef, and a bass with the bass clef, in his fifth symphony. Dvořák usually had two altos and a bass. But nowadays it is customary to have two tenors using a tenor clef, and a bass, though some composers use a bass clef for all three. The range of the tenor

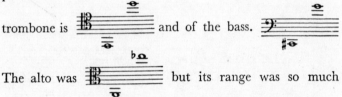

trombone is and of the bass.

The alto was but its range was so much like that of the trumpet that it died out. Alto trombone parts in old scores are now played on the tenor trombone.

Sometimes the three instruments play in unison, as in Wagner's prelude to Act III of 'Lohengrin'; sometimes they play in three-part harmony, as in the Weber extract given on p. 37; and sometimes they make five-part harmony with the two trumpets, with whom they blend very well. They have a noble, powerful tone, and can play both *pp* and *ff*.

Orchestral Scores of the Nineteenth Century

Schubert, Weber, Schumann, Dvořák and Brahms were usually content with the Beethoven orchestra mentioned earlier in this chapter, plus the addition of three trombones. Look at page 37, which is taken from Weber's overture to 'Der Freischütz'. Can you tell whether he is writing for B♭ or A clarinets? He is using four horns, two in E♭ on the top stave, and two in C on the bottom, so as to

WEBER : DER FREISCHÜTZ OVERTURE

(Boosey and Hawkes score, p. 7)

give him more available notes.   Play the horn parts at their
actual pitch on the piano, remembering that horns in C
sound an octave lower than written.   The trumpets are in
C, so do not require transposition.   The clef will tell you
whether Weber is using alto or tenor trombones.   Play the
three trombone parts on the piano.

Chapter Four

Triple Woodwind

There was a tendency throughout the nineteenth century to introduce new instruments into the orchestra, and to increase its size. Composers began to use a smaller flute (the piccolo), a larger oboe (the cor anglais), a larger clarinet (the bass clarinet), and a larger bassoon (the double bassoon). Sometimes the second flute player played the piccolo, the second oboe the cor anglais and so on, for a player can usually play another instrument of the same family. But more often an extra player was used for each of these instruments; and if all four were introduced it meant twelve players, or "triple woodwind": that is, three of each of the four main kinds instead of two.

However, they were not necessarily all introduced in the same score. A composer might want a piccolo or cor anglais for a special effect, and otherwise be content with "double woodwind". Conversely, Wagner or a twentieth-century composer may ask for sixteen woodwind players. Since the middle of last century, there has not been a standard number of woodwind instruments required for orchestral works, comparable to the double woodwind that was common in Beethoven's day, though modern orchestras usually have triple woodwind as their normal establishment.

The Piccolo

The piccolo, whose full name is flauto piccolo, "little flute", is about twelve inches long. Its compass is written

but it actually sounds an octave higher than this. For this reason the Italians sometimes call it

39

"ottavino". It produces the highest sounds in the orchestra, and is so shrill that it can be heard above the noisiest tutti. It has a brilliant, exciting effect.

It is used by Beethoven in the last movement of his fifth symphony, and at the end of his exciting 'Egmont' overture; by Wagner in the forging scene from 'Siegfried' and the 'Ride to the Valkyries'; and by Tschaikowsky in 'Chinese Dance' from the 'Nutcracker' Suite, in the scherzo of his fourth symphony and the ballet 'Swan Lake'. It is clearly heard in variation A of Britten's 'Young Person's Guide to the Orchestra', and you can see how its part is written in the two pages from this work quoted on pp. 53, 54.

The Cor Anglais

The cor anglais is *not* a horn. No one really knows how it got its name, though it is thought that "anglais" may originally have been "anglé", as the instrument had an angle in the middle. Nowadays it is vertical, like the oboe, but it has a curved mouthpiece to make it easier to hold. It also has a larger bell at the bottom than has the oboe.

Its written compass is which is very like that of the oboe without the top notes. But it is a longer instrument, and its actual pitch is a fifth below the oboe and a fifth below its written pitch—which means it is another transposing instrument. This is easy for the player, as it means he can cover the same hole on both oboe and cor anglais and give it the same name, even though it sounds different. But the score reader has always to transpose the cor anglais part down a perfect fifth, in order to discover the exact pitch.

Look at the cor anglais part in the Tschaikowsky score quoted on pp. 46, 47, and play it on the piano at its actual pitch.

The cor anglais has the same throaty tone as the oboe, but it is deeper and even more expressive. It is mainly used for plaintive melodies, such as that at the beginning of the

slow movement of Dvořák's 'New World' symphony.
Franck also uses it for the slow movement of his symphony,
and other famous examples occur in the overtures to Rossini's
'William Tell', Tschaikowsky's 'Romeo and Juliet' and
Wagner's 'Flying Dutchman'.

The Bass Clarinet

The bass clarinet is twice as long as the ordinary clarinet
and therefore sounds an octave lower. Bass clarinets in C,
B♮ and A will be found in nineteenth-century scores, but
only the B♭ size is used today. The written compass is

, but a B♭ instrument sounds a ninth

below this, while a part written for an instrument in A
sounds a tenth lower. But sometimes a bass clef is used,
and then the instruments sound a second and a third lower
than written, like ordinary clarinets.

The modern bass clarinet was designed by Sax, the
inventor of the saxophone; and indeed, with its curved
mouthpiece and upturned bell, it looks rather like one,
except for the fact that the saxophone is always made of metal.
It has the same agility, wide range of dynamics, and tone
quality as the clarinet, but with an even richer, more velvety
tone. It is not in such frequent use as the cor anglais, and
it rarely plays a solo. Listen to it playing a little downward
scale in between the first celesta phrases in Tschaikowsky's
'Dance of the Sugar Plum Fairy'. Then look at the part
shown in the 'Russian Dance', quoted on pp. 46, 47, and
play it on the piano at its actual pitch.

The Double Bassoon

The double or contra bassoon is twice as long as a bassoon,
and is therefore an octave lower. Its compass is written

but, like the double bass, it sounds an

octave lower. It looks like a larger and heavier version of the bassoon, and it is played in the same way. It is a useful addition to the bass section of the orchestra, and its low notes are very powerful. It is rarely heard alone, but Haydn uses it to depict the beasts and the worm in 'The Creation'; its grunts can be heard in Dukas's 'The Sorcerer's Apprentice', and it represents the beast in Ravel's 'Beauty and the Beast' from his 'Mother Goose Suite'. It also occurs in the last movement of Beethoven's fifth and ninth symphonies, and in Brahms's first, third and fourth symphonies and his 'Saint Antony' variations; but although it adds to the sonority, its voice cannot be singled out in these and similar works. Tschaikowsky never used it, but modern English composers write for it quite frequently.

Valve Horns. The Horn in F

Valves were first applied to horns in 1818, but they were not in regular use until the end of the century, for some performers and some conservative composers, such as Brahms, did not think the tone of the valve horn was as good as that of the natural, or "hand" horn. But Schumann and Wagner adopted it quite early, and nowadays it has completely superseded the natural horn.

There are usually three valves, and, as you can see from the photograph, each one lets the air into an extra coil of tube, thus lowering the pitch without having to stop playing to insert extra pieces of tubing into the instrument. The first valve lowers the pitch a semitone, the second one two semitones, and the third one three. You will realise that various combinations of these valves will give any note within a range of an augmented fourth, thus bridging the gap between all the harmonics except the octave between numbers 1 and 2; so that, for the first time, a complete chromatic scale from the second harmonic becomes a possibility. Modern horns sometimes have four valves. The fourth valve shuts off some of the tubing, instead of adding it, and makes the whole instrument sound a fourth higher. The top notes are then easier to produce, as they are lower in the harmonic series.

Horn

Trumpet

Tuba

Timpani

Now that every note was obtainable one might have expected that horn parts would be written at their actual pitch. But no! Makers and players decided that the horn in F was the best size, so composers had to write for this, and the part still sounded a fifth lower than written—which is, of course, what happened in an older work with horn parts in F. The only difference is that, since valve horns have come into use, *all* horn parts are played on an F horn, whatever the key of the movement. And they are still normally written without key signature, though Elgar and a few other composers occasionally add one.

The style of writing has not changed, because the rich, poetic tone quality of the horn is still suited to sonorous melodies, rich chords and throbbing repeated notes. The compass of the valve horn is sounding a fifth lower.

Look at the horn parts given in the Tschaikowsky score on pp. 46, 47, and in the Britten score on pp. 53, 54, and play them on the piano at the correct pitch, that is, a fifth below their written pitch. You will notice that both scores use the standard number of four horns.

The Valve Trumpet

Valves began to be used on trumpets about the same time as on horns, and they work on the same principle. But, unlike the horn, which became standardised in F, trumpets in F, D, C and B♭ were used, the notation being as for the natural trumpet. Nowadays the trumpet in B♭ is the most common size, but parts are often written as for trumpet in C, that is, non-transposing, which means that if the player has a B♭ trumpet *he* has to do the transposing, rather than the reader. As far as score reading is concerned, it is clear from the information at the beginning of the score, whether the part is transposing or not. It is usual to show the key signature in modern trumpet parts. The compass of the modern trumpet is .

In the Tschaikowsky score quoted on pp. 46, 47, the trumpets are in A, and are therefore treated just as they would be in a Beethoven score: that is, the sound is a third lower. But in the Britten score on pp. 53, 54, the part is written for trumpets in C, which means that they are non-transposing, and are written in the key of the piece, like the violins, using a key signature where necessary.

The Tuba

Horns and trombones do not go as low as a double bass, and there has always been a need for a good bass instrument in the brass section. At one time, some members of the now obsolete cornett (not cornet) family were tried for this purpose. They were a cross between woodwind and brass instruments, as they had a cup mouthpiece, like that of a trumpet, and finger holes like those of an oboe. The serpent was eight feet long, and was coiled like its namesake. Mendelssohn used this in his oratorio 'St Paul'. The ophicleide was bent back on itself like a bassoon, and Mendelssohn tried it out in his overture 'A Midsummer Night's Dream'. But eventually they were all superseded by the tuba, a new kind of valved instrument, which came into use about the same time that valves were invented for trumpets and horns.

There is a whole family of tubas. The small ones are called euphoniums and are much used for solo work in brass bands. But the bass tuba in F is the one that has made itself useful in orchestras. Its compass is

and it is non-transposing. Berlioz and Wagner were two of the first composers to use it.

It looks rather like a horn, and has a similar mechanism, but its bell points upward and it is very large. Its tone is more like that of the horn than the trombone, and it gets rather gruff and coarse when playing loudly, as it lacks the metallic edge of trombone tone. There is usually only one tuba in an orchestra and it acts as a bass to either horns or trombone, often playing an octave below their bass line, just as double basses play an octave below the 'cellos.

It is only heard by itself when it is wanted for some special effect, as in 'The Bear walking on his hind Legs' from Stravinsky's 'Petrouchka'. When Strauss wants to poke fun at critics in his 'Ein Heldenleben' he has two tubas playing a pair of consecutive fifths a semitone apart, thus,

, and very comical they sound.

The tuba usually shares a stave with the bass trombone, as in the Tschaikowsky score quoted on pp. 46, 47. It is not specially indicated on p. 47, but it plays the bottom G throughout this line, while the bass trombone plays the top note on the stave. In the Britten score on pp. 53, 54, however, you will see it has a stave to itself.

Reading a Tschaikowsky Score

Look down the names of the instruments at the side of the first page of the score, printed on p. 46, translating them into English, noting their key signatures and transpositions, and reminding yourself of their sound and methods of performance. Then look at the music. The strings have both the tune and the harmonies, but notice how the woodwind and horns reinforce them. Try to hear the effect or to play it on the piano.

Then compare it with the second page, when the whole orchestra is playing. The tune is now in three octaves in the strings, as well as in flutes and clarinets; but the brass is also very busy, and certainly adds to the excitement. After studying these two pages (which are pages 42 and 51 in the Boosey and Hawkes score) listen to the whole piece on the gramophone while following the complete score. If possible, hear it three times, following the strings, woodwind and brass groups in turn.

TSCHAIKOWSKY : CASSE NOISETTE SUITE
(*Boosey and Hawkes score, p. 42*)

DANSE RUSSE
Trepak

(Boosey and Hawkes score, p. 51)

Chapter Five

Percussion Instruments

In addition to the timpani, which are used in all kinds of orchestral music and which produce notes of exact pitch, there are many other percussion instruments which are used for special effects. If they have no exact pitch it is customary to write their parts on one line instead of five, so as to save space.

There are many kinds of drum, but the two most common are the big bass drum with its deep throbbing note, and the small side or "snare" drum with its high-pitched rat-tat-tat. Then there are cymbals, castanets, tambourines and gongs, which you probably know quite well. And composers may use anything else they wish for a special effect, from a whip to a wind machine.

Further effects can be obtained by hitting the instruments with different kinds of sticks, or setting them in motion in various other ways. Drums can also be muffled by draping them with a cloth. Beethoven in his 'Ruins of Athens' writes: "At this point add all the noisy instruments possible, castanets, cymbals, etc.", so programme effects of this kind go quite a long way back in history.

There is a tambourine part in the Tschaikowsky score shown on pp. 46, 47, and it is put to effective use on p. 47. The Britten quotation on p. 54 uses cymbals, bass drum, tambourine and side drum. Look at their notation. Variation M in this work also brings in the triangle, gong, castanets, chinese block and whip. It is exciting to hear, but even more exciting to see in the concert hall!

In recent years some percussion instruments with a definite pitch have come into orchestral use. The main ones are mentioned below.

The Tubular Bells

These consist of long metal tubes hung in a wooden frame and struck by hammers. They sound rather like church bells. Sometimes a composer uses one or two for a bell-like effect, at other times a complete scale is required. The best-known example of the latter is in Tschaikowsky's '1812' overture.

The Glockenspiel

Another bell-like instrument is the glockenspiel. It consists of a series of small metal bars arranged in the same order as a piano keyboard, and they are struck by hammers.

The written compass is but it sounds an octave or even two octaves higher than this. Some makers have connected the metal bars to a keyboard, so that the instrument can be played like a piano. Papageno's magic instrument in Mozart's 'Magic Flute' is a glockenspiel. Wagner uses it effectively in the 'Dance of the Apprentices', from 'The Mastersingers', and in the "fire" music from 'The Valkyrie'; and Tschaikowsky uses it in the 'Chinese Dance' from the 'Nutcracker' suite

The Celesta

The celesta also consists of metal bars, but it has wooden resonators in addition, and it is always played by means of a keyboard. It looks rather like a small upright piano, but it is much more bell-like and liquid in tone. Its compass is written but it sounds an octave higher, and its part is written on two staves, like piano music.

The first famous instance of its use is in Tschaikowsky's 'Dance of the Sugar Plum Fairy', but it is quite frequently used by modern composers for special effects.

4

The Xylophone

This also consists of a series of bars with resonators, and it looks a little like a glockenspiel; but the bars are made of hard wood, and the tone is quite different, being hard and brilliant instead of liquid and bell-like. The usual compass is ![musical notation: staff with 8va marking]. The xylophone and its close relative the marimba, both come from Asia and Africa. You will see a few notes for the xylophone on the Britten score quoted on p. 54.

The Harp

The harp is not really a percussion instrument, although it is grouped with them in the score. It is the only plucked string instrument in regular use in the orchestra. Although it is very ancient it is only comparatively recently that it has come into the orchestra. The compass is ![musical notation: bass and treble staff] and its part is written on two staves, like piano music.

The harp has seven strings to each octave, one for each letter name. It also has seven pedals, one for each letter name, and each of them can alter the pitch of all its own set of notes throughout the instrument, one pedal altering all the As, another all the Bs and so on. Each pedal has three positions. When it is in the top notch all the strings it affects sound as flats; if it is half-way down the strings are tightened up to naturals; and when fully depressed the strings become sharps. The pedals can thus be set for any desired key. For example, the key of D will have the F and C pedals fully depressed and the others at the half-way position.

You must have noticed how often harpists play glissando (a rapid gliding over every string). They can glissando any scale with ease. Look at the first quoted page of the Britten score on p.53. The harpist has been told on the previous page to set his strings for the scale of D♭ major, and you will see that he has two glissandos to execute in the first four bars. Harpists can also play glissando chords by setting the pedals so that two strings play the same note. Work out how the pedals could be set so as to play this chord glissando throughout the whole range of the instrument.

Chords are usually played "arpeggio" which means "like a harp", and harmonics are as effective on the harp as on the violin. One or two harps are often required in a modern orchestra, and occasionally even more are wanted for a special effect, as, for example, when Wagner requires six for the 'Entry of the Gods into Valhalla' in his 'Rhinegold'. The last movement of Tschaikowsky's 'Nutcracker' suite, the 'Waltz of the Flowers', opens with a harp cadenza. The harp is very popular with impressionist composers such as Debussy and Ravel. It is used most effectively in Debussy's 'L'Après-midi d'un Faune'.

The Large Modern Orchestra

A composer who uses every instrument described in these chapters requires such an expensive orchestra that concert promoters will think twice before performing his works today. Wagner asked for a large orchestra with triple or even quadruple woodwind and heavy brass, and the tendency up to the 1914 war was to demand increasingly large orchestras. Strauss, Holst and Elgar are three composers to whom this applies. But although composers such as Vaughan Williams and Walton may still require a large orchestra on occasion today, there has also been a tendency recently to use smaller forces, sometimes for rather unusual combinations.

The standard orchestra today usually has triple woodwind, four horns, three trumpets, three trombones, tuba, timpani, two or three other percussion players, harp and strings, and this often makes about eighty players. Other players are then brought in as required.

The score quoted on pp. 53, 54, does not employ very large forces, though it is well supplied with percussion. The names of the instruments are clearly shown at the beginning of every line. It is scored for double woodwind plus piccolo, and the usual brass. The timpani, xylophone, other percussion parts and harp come next in the score. You will see that the timpani are to be played with wooden sticks and that the composer has put "tambourine ad lib." in a footnote, in case there are not enough percussion players available. Which instruments have the most important themes at L and which at M?

BRITTEN: THE YOUNG PERSON'S GUIDE TO THE ORCHESTRA

(*Boosey and Hawkes score, p. 60*)

(Boosey and Hawkes score, p. 61)

PART TWO

MUSICAL FORM

Chapter Six

(More detailed information concerning the facts given in this chapter, together with musical examples, will be found in the author's *Melody Writing and Analysis*.)

Phrase Structure

The unit of thought in music in the *phrase*. "Phrase" is a very loose term, and the length can be anything from one to eight bars. Perhaps the most usual length is four bars. Two, four and eight bars are much more common than three, five and seven. It is usual to say that a phrase must end with a cadence, but a four-bar phrase may divide into halves with a cadence at the end of each half, and in such a case some people may consider it is two phrases, not one. The exact terminology is unimportant.

When two or more phrases come to a main stopping place with a reasonably finished perfect or plagal cadence they are said to form a *sentence*. It is even possible for one phrase to form a sentence in itself.

Phrases often divide into smaller parts, which are usually called *sections*. A four-bar phrase often divides into two sections of equal length. A section may divide again, into shorter *figures* or *units*, which are often of one bar's length.

The following tune consists of a complete sentence divided into two phrases of four bars. The first phrase contains two units of one bar each and a section of two bars; and the second phrase consists of two sections of two bars each.

Barbara Allen

Repetition

Music is a language, but it lacks the exact meaning, clarity and logic of words, and therefore it requires more repetition than verbal language does, in order to avoid incoherence and produce any recognisable shape.

The most common shape for a sixteen-bar melody is A A B A, as in 'All through the Night'. But repetition is just as essential in large-scale works. It is most important, in listening to music, to cultivate a good memory, otherwise the composer's repetitions are missed, and the music appears shapeless.

Sequence

Repetition is not bound to be exact, and in fact it rarely is so, in more highly evolved music. A common variant is the repetition of a phrase at a higher or lower pitch, and, providing that it follows on immediately, this is called a *sequence*. A sequence may be melodic (in the melody only) or harmonic (complete harmonies also), and it may be exact or slightly modified.

Augmentation and Diminution

Some or all of the notes of a phrase may be repeated in longer notes, *augmentation*, or in shorter notes, *diminution*. These devices are particularly common in fugues, but they frequently occur elsewhere. The finale of Elgar's 'Enigma' variations contains an augmentation of 'Nimrod', and there are frequent cases of diminution in the first and last movements of Dvořák's 'New World' symphony.

Variation, Ornamentation and Development

There are many other ways of varying the repetition of a phrase to make it more interesting. Slight differences may produce a "varied repetition"; or additional ornamentation may be added to the melody or accompaniment, as in many variations of the earlier classical composers, such as Handel's 'Harmonious Blacksmith' or Schubert's 'Impromptu in B♭'.

Other methods of varying a repeat can all come under the heading "development". The intervals in a melody may be changed while the rhythm is recognisably the same; or every interval in a melody may go in the opposite direction, which is called *melodic inversion*. Sometimes part of a phrase only may be developed, as for example when a rhythmic figure is repeated, perhaps working up to a climax. The key may be changed, the harmonies may be varied, the scoring of an orchestral work may be different while the theme is recognisably the same. All these devices contribute to the unity of a work and give it coherence and shape.

Contrast

But contrast is just as necessary, in order to prevent monotony. A composition is satisfactory in its form if it has a satisfying balance between unity (created by various forms of repetition) and contrast, whatever the shape or the length of the work may be.

Contrast of melody may be produced by a different melodic shape or style, or by a contrasted rhythm. A contrasted style of accompaniment is another possibility; or there may be contrasts of key, dynamics, speed, orchestration and so on. Naturally a larger work, or movement from a work, can stand more sharp contrasts than can a small one.

It has become customary to label contrasting *themes* by letters, A, B, and so on. But such letters are also often used for different *sections* of a work, even though they may contain a good deal of repetition. For example, binary form (see Chapter Eight) is often called A B, but the second section usually contains far more repetition than contrast. It is important, therefore, to realise that someone else may use letters in quite a different way, when describing the same movement, and both methods may be equally correct. If you use such letters you must make it clear what you mean by them. To say that C returns is quite pointless unless you have previously stated what *you* are calling C.

Subjects and Episodes

A theme which occurs more than once is called a *subject*. A theme which only occurs *once* is called an *episode*. Episodes occur in many types of harmonic forms. But the word "episode" has a different meaning in fugue (see Chapter Seven.)

Contrast of Key

Contrast of key is at least as important as contrast of theme, and modulation is one of the chief ways of getting variety into a composition. There are cases, as, for example, in the first movement of Haydn's 'London' symphony, where the second subject is the same as the first, but in a contrasted key, the dominant.

The dominant is the most natural and usual contrasted key for a piece of music in the major mode, while the relative major is the most common for a piece in the minor. This applies to a simple song like 'The Bluebells of Scotland' just as much as to a Beethoven symphony. But whereas a short song may contain just one modulation, a symphonic movement will contain a large number. The skill of the composer is shown in the balance he achieves in his key scheme.

It is customary to modulate to keys on the sharp side of the tonic in the first part of a movement, and to the flat side towards the end. The earlier classical composers kept to the most closely related keys, but Beethoven and Schubert began to be more adventurous, and *any* key is possible if the composer can make the tonality into a coherent, satisfying whole.

The return to the tonic key is one of the most important ways of achieving unity, and however far afield a composer ventures, he must make the listener feel he has returned home when he reaches the tonic key again. Even the most modern piece of music begins and ends on the same tonic, though it may perhaps begin in the minor mode and end in the major. Changes of key are quite as important as changes of theme, and the main modulations should always be stated, when writing out an analysis.

Pedal

A device in common use in all kinds of music is that of *pedal*. One note is held, or repeated either in plain or in decorated form, while the music continues with harmonies of which the pedal may play no part.

Tonic and dominant pedals are the most common. The dominant often effectively leads to a climax, producing a desire for the return to the tonic, while a tonic pedal often has a quietening effect at the end of a piece. Pedals are usually in the bass. If they occur in an upper part they are termed *inverted pedals*.

Extension and Contraction of Phrase

Phrases are quite frequently extended and this often happens after a regular four bar phrase rhythm has been established, thus providing a delightful variation of the prevailing pattern. Phrases may be extended by repetition or sequence; by augmentation; by interpolation of an extra bar or two; by cadential extension or repetition; and so on.

Contraction of phrases is less common. It may occur by diminution, or by letting the last note of one phrase overlap with the first note of the next. Sometimes no reason can be given for the contraction; a phrase just *is* three bars instead of four. The ear expects the normal four bars and is usually conscious of the irregularity.

Coda and Codetta

A *coda* is a passage which rounds off a piece of music, giving it greater finality. It may be of any length, from a few bars to several pages; and it may contain new material, or a further development of the old.

A *codetta* is a little coda, and the term is usually applied to the ending of a *section* of a movement or piece.   (It has a different meaning in fugue—see p. 66.)

Chapter Seven

Musical Texture

Melody consists of a single line of music.

Counterpoint consists of two or more lines of music, so arranged as to fit well together. This means that they must make satisfactory harmony, even though the combination of melodies is the main aim. *Polyphony* is another word meaning the same thing.

In contrapuntal writing it is customary to call each melodic line a "voice part", whether it is written for a voice or an instrument.

Harmony is a series of chords which sound well in succession. The melodic parts which produce the harmony will also make counterpoint with each other, but in a harmonic style of writing the contrapuntal interest is secondary. *Homophony* is another word meaning the same thing.

It will be seen, therefore, that except in the case of a single melodic line, all composition consists of a mixture of harmony and counterpoint. In the days of the earliest vocal writers, such as the Elizabethan madrigalists, the emphasis was on the contrapuntal texture. Bach and Handel were more conscious of the harmony, but their music was still contrapuntal, so they achieved a good balance between the two. After this came a period when the interest shifted much more to harmonic styles and forms, so that the sonatas and symphonies of Haydn, Mozart and Beethoven are predominantly harmonic, though even here there are passages where counterpoint comes to the fore. Wagner, for all his richness of harmony, often combines themes in counterpoint; and the most satisfying type of composition is that which contains both harmonic and contrapuntal interest.

Contrapuntal Forms

Forms based on a contrapuntal texture come historically before the harmonic forms. Contrapuntal forms are mainly concerned with the texture from bar to bar, while harmonic forms depend more upon contrasts of theme and key, which produce a definite shape in a large scale design. For example, an Elizabethan madrigal begins with one musical idea which is taken up by all the voices in turn; then, perhaps with the next line of words, goes on to treat another musical idea in the same way; and so on, to the end. There is no deliberately contrasted section or key, and no return to an earlier idea, as one would find in a symphonic movement by Beethoven.

Imitation

A common device used in contrapuntal texture is that of *imitation*. This consists of an idea "sung" by one "voice", and repeated immediately by another voice. The imitation may be exact in every detail; or it may be at a higher or lower pitch; or the intervals may be modified (e.g., d m s might be imitated by m s d¹ or r s t); or it may be inverted (e.g., d m s might be imitated by l f r) and so on. Anything is possible as long as it is recognisable as imitation of the original.

Early Musical Compositions

The earliest written European music is that of *Gregorian chant* or *plainsong*, a single line of melody used for the words of the mass or some other part of the church service. It has the free rhythm of speech, it uses the old church modes, and it is still heard in Roman Catholic churches today.

In the ninth and tenth centuries it became the custom to sing the plainsong tune in four pitches at the same time, to suit treble, alto, tenor and bass voices. The result was a series of consecutive fourths, fifths and octaves. It was the first attempt at harmony, and was called *organum*.

Round about A.D. 1000 the monks began to add independent counterpoints to the traditional plainsong melody. As the plainsong was fixed it was called the *canto fermo*, and the added part was called a *descant*. The added parts gradually became more free in the intervals and the rhythms they used, and often they imitated either the canto fermo plainsong in quicker notes, or each other.

By the sixteenth century composers began to be able to manage without the prop of a plainsong. The parts became of equal importance, and they moved freely in counterpoint, often imitating each other.

The climax of this polyphonic style came with Palestrina in Italy and Byrd and other composers in England. *Motets* and *madrigals* of this period are frequently sung today, and are available on gramophone records. They still use the old modes, and are rather similar in style except that the motet is a sacred composition with Latin words while the madrigal is secular. They are both unaccompanied choral compositions containing a good deal of imitation, and they usually treat each new line of words with a different musical figure.

The *ayre* was less contrapuntal in style than the madrigal and used the same music for each verse of the words. The *ballet* was similar, but rather more dance-like, and had a fa-la refrain at the end of each verse.

Canonic Forms

A *canon* is a piece of contrapuntal music in which one voice repeats the part of another, not just for the opening few notes as with imitation, but throughout the piece or section. The second voice answers the first at half a bar, one bar, two bars or any other distance the composer wishes;

and having started its particular kind of imitation, it keeps it up throughout with exactitude.

But there are many possible methods of imitation in a canon, such as imitation at the octave or fourth or fifth, imitation by inversion, or even imitation which starts at the end and works backwards like a crab, called *canon cancrizans*! And there may, for example, be two parts imitated by another two parts, known as canon 4 in 2. Further details can be obtained from a larger text-book on form.

A *round* is a vocal canon "at the unison", in which the end goes back (round) to the beginning. It can therefore be repeated as often as wished, being an "infinite canon". One of the earliest rounds is 'Sumer is i-cumen in', though it also contains an accompanying ground bass. Rounds were popular in Elizabethan days, and Shakespeare has several in his plays. 'Three blind Mice' dates from this period.

A *catch* is a round with humorous or ribald words. Often the humour is produced by puns or by the juxtaposition of two lines of words heard at the same time. 'Would you know my Celia's Charms' makes great play with her age.

Invertible Counterpoint

This is a contrapuntal combination of melodies so devised that they sound equally well whichever voice is heard at the top or bottom. It is particularly useful in fugue. If two parts are concerned it is called *double* counterpoint, if three *triple* counterpoint, and so on. The inversion is usually at the octave, but it can be at the tenth or twelfth.

Fugue

A fugue is a piece of music of contrapuntal texture which is mainly based on one theme, called the subject. It is very free in form—some authorities prefer to call it a texture rather than a form. But it begins by establishing a tonic key (*the exposition*), has a section which modulates away from it (*the middle section*), and finally re-establishes the tonic (*final section*). It is important to realise that the divisions correspond to contrasts of key rather than of theme, and that fugue is really one indivisible whole.

It is most usually written for three or four voices, but two or five or even more are possible, though it is hard for the listener to distinguish even four strands of melody at the same time.

A pictorial analysis of an imaginary simple fugue in three parts is shown on p. 67, and this, together with the definitions of technical terms given below, should be sufficient to give an understanding of the main principles. Fugue must, of course, be studied in relation to actual examples. Bach was the great master of fugue, and if no particular fugue has to be studied for examination purposes, fugue no. 2 of his '48' will provide a clear and simple illustration of the main features. Handel also has some fine fugues in his 'Messiah'.

Subject (*S*). This is the main theme, which is first heard in one voice alone (unless a vocal fugue happens to have an independent instrumental accompaniment.) It is usually quite short and easily remembered.

Answer (*A*). This is the *same* theme as the subject but sung a fifth higher or fourth lower to suit a different kind of voice. The voices usually enter with subject and answer alternately.

If the subject is entirely in the tonic key and the answer is an exact transposition it will therefore be in the dominant key and will be called a *real* answer. But frequently it is modified and is then called a *tonal* answer. For example, if the subject starts doh soh it usually sounds better to let the answer start soh doh¹ instead of soh ray . Similarly soh doh¹ at or near the beginning is usually answered by doh¹ soh¹, not doh¹ fah¹, and the result in both cases may well be that the answer will begin and even remain in the tonic key. (See fugue 17 of the '48'.) Another kind of tonal answer occurs if the subject modulates to the dominant key. The answer is then modified so as to return from the dominant to the tonic key. (See fugue 7 of the '48'.) It is easy to tell whether an answer is real or tonal by seeing if the transposition is exact or not.

Counter subject (*C.S.*). When a voice has sung the subject or

5

answer it continues with another figure. It can be a different tune every time if the composer wishes, but if it is the same on each occasion it is called a counter subject. It should work equally well whether it is sung above or below the subject or answer, and therefore needs to be in double counterpoint.

Free part. A voice which is not singing the subject or counter subject is said to have a "free part". It is often based on figures derived from the S or C.S.

Codetta. Sometimes, in order to avoid monotony, there is a few bars' delay before the next voice enters with S or A, and all the voices which have already entered have free parts. If this occurs in the exposition it is called a codetta. (The term has a different meaning in harmonic forms, such as sonata form.) See fugue no. 2 of the '48', bars 5–7.

Exposition. The voices can enter in any order, and the exposition normally comes to an end when all the voices have entered with either S or A.

Redundant Entry. But sometimes one of the voices enters again with S or A before the fugue begins to modulate away from tonic and dominant keys. The reason for this is usually to give an opportunity for S and C.S. to be inverted in relation to each other. Look at the plan on p. 67. If the exposition stopped after the entry of the third voice, the listener would not have heard the C.S. above the S. The redundant entry makes this possible. See fugue no. 7 of the '48', where there is a redundant entry in the soprano.

Counter exposition. Sometimes all the voices enter again with S and A before modulating into the middle section. In such a counter exposition, the voices which previously had the subject will now have the answer, and vice versa. See no. 9 of the '48', bars 6–10. In a partial counter exposition some, but not all, of the voices re-enter.

Middle section. When the music begins to move away from tonic and dominant keys it has reached the middle section. There is no clear-cut cadence or division between the sections, but it is usual to consider that the middle section starts after the last note of the last entry of S or A in tonic or dominant key.

Episode. An episode is the same thing as a codetta (i.e. all voices having free parts), but the term "codetta" is confined to the exposition. Elsewhere in a fugue it is called an episode. The middle section usually begins and ends with an episode, but episodes can occur anywhere in a fugue after the exposition, and there can be as many or as few as the composer wishes. Their purpose is to make a change from too frequent entries of the subject, and to provide a modulatory link. But they do not consist of completely new material as in harmonic forms such as episodical and rondo. They are usually based on some figure from the S or C.S.

AN IMAGINARY FUGUE IN THREE PARTS

Voice	Exposition				Middle Section				Final Section			Coda
Soprano		Sub. ∿∿	F.P.	C.S. ✕✕✕✕	F.P.	Sub. (M.E.) ∿∿	C.S. ✕✕✕✕	F.P.	F.P.	Sub. ∿∿	F.P.	a d o C
Alto	Ans. ∿∿	C.S. ✕✕✕✕	*Codetta* F.P.	*Episode* F.P.	Ans. (M.E.) ∿∿	*Episode* F.P.	F.P. Sub. ∿∿	F.P.	F.P.			o C
Bass	Sub. ∿∿	C.S. ✕✕✕✕	F.P.	Sub. (R.E.) ∿∿	*Episode* C.S. ✕✕✕✕	F.P.	*Episode* Sub.	F.P.	Sub. (augmentation) ∿∿			Tonic pedal

Sub. ∿∿ = subject. Ans. ∿∿ = answer. R.E. ∿∿ = redundant entry. M.E. ∿∿ = middle entry.

C.S. ✕✕✕✕ = counter subject. F.P. ---- = free part.

Middle Entries. In the middle section, entries of the subject occur in keys other than the tonic and dominant, in between the episodes. They are usually in related keys; they can enter singly, or in pairs as S and A; and there can be as many or as few middle entries as the composer wishes.

Final Section. The final section begins when one of the voices brings the subject back in the tonic key. The composer can make this section as long or as short as he likes, and can introduce the subject in as many or as few voices as he likes.

Coda. If the music continues after the last note of the last entry of the subject, the rest of the music will form a coda. See the last two bars of fugue 1 of the '48'.

Other features. Sometimes one voice enters with S or A before the previous voice has finished, thus heightening the tension. This device is called *stretto.* It may occur between any number of voices and in any part of the fugue, though it is more usual towards the end. Fugue no. 1 of the '48' is full of stretti. The subject may also be heard in *augmentation* (see fugue 8 of the '48', bars 62–67), or *diminution* (see fugue 33 of the '48', bars 26–29), or *by inversion* (see fugue 16, bars 14, 22 and 27). A dominant or tonic *pedal* is frequently heard towards the end of a fugue, particularly in the bass (see fugue 2 of the '48', last three bars).

Double fugue. Fugues are occasionally written with two subjects. They may occur together at the beginning, or each may have a separate exposition before being combined.

Fugato

Fugato means "in fugal style". Many movements in harmonic forms such as sonata form may have a fugato passage, which starts like the exposition of a fugue, but does not continue in the style. Fugatos also occur in choral and operatic works.

Chapter Eight

Binary Form

Binary form, as its name implies, is two part form.   But it is necessary to avoid two common misapprehensions:— (1) the two parts are not necessarily equal in length: the second part is frequently much longer than the first; (2) the two parts are often designated A and B but this does not mean that they consist of two different themes.   The second section is almost invariably built on the same idea(s) as the first.

'Barbara Allen' and 'The Keel Row' are two obvious examples of this form on a very simple scale.   Nearly all the dances in Bach's suites are in binary form, and it is also frequently used for small sections of larger pieces or movements.

A very short, simple example of binary form may stay in the tonic key throughout, and a few of the slightest of Bach's dances do this.   But usually he ends the first part with a perfect cadence in a related key.   If the dance is in a major key, this complementary key is the dominant major; if a minor key, it is sometimes the relative major, but much more frequently it is the dominant minor, ending with a *tierce de Picardie*, so as to make an easy return to the tonic.

The second part frequently starts with the same idea as the opening and returns to the tonic key.   It is usually longer than the first part, it may contain several modulations to related keys, and it sometimes includes a little development.   Often the cadence bars of the two parts are similar except for the change of key.

The Dances of the Suite

The Elizabethans used to pair a slow dance (the *pavane*) with a quick one (the *galliard*.)   Many such sets will be found in 'The Fitzwilliam Virginal Book'. Gradually the idea of collecting a set of dances in the same key to make a longer whole became customary. The English called the collection a *suite* or *lesson*; the French a *suite* or *ordre*; the Germans a *Partita* and the Italians a *sonata da camera*, thus distinguishing a chamber sonata containing secular dances from a *sonata da chiesa*, a church sonata without dances. "Suite" and "sonata" in these early days meant practically the same thing: that is, a collection of instrumental movements; though a sonata was sometimes a one-movement piece.

By the time of Bach and Handel the suite had become rather standardised. It consisted of a set of dances which were almost invariably in binary form. They were all in the same key, though this seems monotonous to us today. The only exception to this was that if there was a pair of dances of the same kind, as for example two minuets or two gavottes, the second one was sometimes in the tonic or relative major or minor.

There were four standard dances which occurred in the same order. They were:

Allemande. This was probably of German origin. It was in $\frac{4}{4}$ time, beginning with an anacrusis of one or three semiquavers. It was of moderate speed, and usually had a continuous semiquaver flow.

Courante. There were two forms of this dance. The French courante was in running $\frac{3}{2}$ time with its cadences in $\frac{6}{4}$, therefore producing a cross rhythm effect. It usually had contrapuntally weaving parts. The Italian *corrente* was quicker and less contrapuntal and was in $\frac{3}{4}$ time.

Sarabande. This was of Spanish origin. It was in a slow and stately triple time, and more harmonic in style than the other dances. It often had a strong accent on the second beat of the bar.

Gigue. This dance originally came from the British Isles, where it was called a jig. The French called it gigue and the Italians giga, and it became the final dance of the suite. It was quick and gay and usually in compound time, with a "skipping" sort of rhythm. It often opened in fugato style, and the second part frequently started with an inversion of the same figure.

In between the sarabande and the gigue composers often introduced several other dances in a lighter and simpler harmonic style, such as:

Minuet. This was a stately French dance in triple time. Sometimes it was followed by a second minuet. This was later called a trio, because it was customary in orchestral music to write it for three instruments only. The first minuet was then repeated.

Gavotte. This was another stately French dance, but in ⁴⁄₄ or ²⁄₂ time, with each phrase starting at the half bar. This was sometimes followed by a second gavotte. If the latter was built over a pedal it was called a *musette*, after the French bagpipe of that name. The first gavotte was then repeated.

Bourrée. This was similar to the gavotte except that each phrase started on the last quarter of the bar.

Passepied. This was a gay French dance in triple time, beginning on the last beat of the bar.

Sometimes the suite began with some sort of prelude which was not in a dance form.

Between 1650 and 1750 Bach was one of the few composers who kept to the same formal arrangement of the dances in his suites, though most composers introduced an allemande and a courante. Purcell introduced short dances, some of them, such as the hornpipe, not found in the suites of other composers. Handel sometimes included sets of variations while Couperin delighted in giving his pieces colourful titles such as "Butterflies" and "Little Windmills". The many fine 'sonatas' of Scarlatti are related to the movements of the suite but often cannot be labelled as any particular dance; nor were they organised into suites.

But although the classical suite almost died out after 1750, more recent composers still occasionally write suites, and a modern suite can be a collection of almost any kind of movements. It may imitate the classical suite, as in Grieg's 'Holberg' suite, or be a collection of dances from a ballet, such as Tschaikowsky's 'Nutcracker' suite, or a series of movements from a play, as in Grieg's 'Peer Gynt'. The movements are in different keys, and the composer is free to use any form he chooses.

Variation Form

When composers first began to write instrumental music in the sixteenth century they were conscious of the need for form, but hardly knew how to construct a piece of any length.   So they fell back on songs and dances as foundations on which to build their instrumental pieces.   Byrd wrote many sets of pavanes and galliards.   But in order to produce a longer piece he frequently wrote variations on a song-like tune or a dance.   There is, for example, a fine set of variations on 'Sellenger's Round'.   The general plan was for each variation to be more ornate than the last.

A later example is the air and variations from Handel's fifth harpsichord suite in E major, popularly known as 'The Harmonious Blacksmith'.   Here the tune is clearly in binary form.   The variations are known as "doubles".   The first two decorate the quaver tune and the chord scheme in semiquavers in right and left hand alternately; the next two do the same in semiquaver triplets; and the final variation consists of *vivacissimo* scales.

· Variation form was popular with both Haydn and Mozart, and one movement of a sonata or other instrumental work was frequently in this form.   The theme was usually binary, but was occasionally the kind of extended binary referred to in the next chapter.   The variations sometimes changed from major to minor and vice versa, but they usually still kept quite close to the original theme and chord scheme.

Beethoven and Schubert write some fine variations, too. You may know Schubert's 'Impromptu in B♭', in which he changes the key as well as the mode in one variation and leaves the tune altogether, although he keeps the harmonic scheme.   He finishes with a short coda which refers to the theme in its original form, a common ending at this time.

Brahms was another great variation writer, but if you study his 'Variations on the St Antony Chorale' you will frequently find it hard to detect the link between the theme and a particular variation, though the chord scheme is usually very similar, and new themes or rhythmic figures may be built over it.   As this is an orchestral work Brahms is able to vary the tonal colour as well as the speed and the time signature.   Elgar's 'Enigma' variations is another very fine and well-known work in this form.

The Ground Bass

The *ground bass* consists of a set of variations on a "ground", that is, a bass continuously repeated with varied upper parts.   The form is at least as old as that of variations on a melody.   The ground itself is usually from four to eight bars long.   Byrd wrote a well-known set of variations on a ground called 'The Bells', and Purcell frequently made use of this form.   Perhaps his best-known example is the song 'When I am laid in Earth' from 'Dido and Aeneas', but there are several grounds in this opera.

A *chaconne* and a *passacaglia* are two old dances in triple time based on a ground.   They came from Spain or Italy, and are practically indistinguishable.   Occasionally the bass is transferred to an upper part in one of the repetitions. The variations are sometimes called *couplets*.

The last movement of Beethoven's 'Eroica' symphony begins with a ground and two variations, but a delightful melody appears in variation three, and from then onwards the bass and the melody are used in a very free kind of double variation form, in a most masterly way.   The last movement of Brahms's fourth symphony is also based on a ground; and the finale of his 'St Antony' variations consists of a five bar ground (which is here called a *basso ostinato*) based on the opening phrase of the original theme.

Rondo Form

This is another old form, originally based on the *rondel* or *rondeau* in verse, in which one line or section kept recurring, rather like a chorus.

Couperin wrote many rondos, in which a short theme alternated with quite a number of different episodes, which he called *couplets*.

Gradually the number of episodes became less, and we find that Haydn and Mozart, who frequently used the form for their last movements, based their rondos on the plan A B A C A. The main theme is usually tuneful, sometimes in binary form, and is in the tonic key at every appearance, though it may be varied in some way. The episodes are well contrasted, and in keys other than the tonic. B is usually in a key on the sharp side of the tonic, and C often on the flat side, though it is sometimes in an unrelated key. The sections are sometimes joined by links. A clear example which you may know is the vivace from Beethoven's sonata, opus 79—though Beethoven rarely used this old and simple kind of rondo form.

Ritornello Form

A ritornello is a "little return". The word was used in the seventeenth and early eighteenth centuries to describe recurring instrumental interludes in a vocal work. (Sometimes the word "symphony" is used for the same thing.)

It was also used in the same period to describe the orchestral "tutti" passages in a concerto grosso (see p. 12). The first movement of such a work usually started with a "tutti", after which the soloists came to the fore, either with new material, or, more often, with ideas based upon or linked up with the opening ritornello. The same ritornello tutti occurred at intervals during the movement, separated by passages in which the soloists were predominant, and this plan has been called *ritornello form*.

It was rather like a rondo, but the interludes were more often based on the opening ritornello than really contrasted to it, and the ritornello was not confined to appearances in the tonic key. It frequently occurred in the dominant, then the subdominant, and perhaps also the relative minor or some other key, before making its final appearance in the tonic. The plan was also more unified than the sectional rondo form, and it is frequently impossible to dissect such a movement into regular sections.

This form is well exemplified in the opening movement of Bach's second Brandenburg concerto.

Instrumental Works of the Seventeenth and Early Eighteenth Centuries

The *suite* has already been described, and the distinction has been made between the *sonata da camera* which contained dance forms, and the *sonata da chiesa* which, being church music, did not contain dances but was in other respects the same. The church sonata was the ancestor of the sonata of Mozart and Beethoven.

The term *sonata* (Italian *sonare*, to sound) was originally used in contrast to *cantata* (Italian *cantare*, to sing), and was applied to instrumental music. The most common type of sonata was for strings and continuo (see p. 8), and was usually in four movements, of contrasted speeds but in the same key. The majority of the movements were in binary form, but there would be an occasional one of a fugal character, or even an air with variations. (Sonata form, described on p. 81, had not yet been evolved.)

Corelli and Purcell wrote many string sonatas, while D. Scarlatti wrote harpsichord sonatas which were usually in only one movement. After this period it became the custom to restrict the word sonata to works for only one or two instruments.

The *concerto* (Latin, *concertus* from *certare*, to strive) was a work for a combination of unequal forces, such as voices and instruments, or solo and tutti instrumental groups. The former meaning died out fairly soon, and the concerto became an instrumental work.

Corelli, Bach and Handel usually wrote their concertos for a group of solo instruments ("concertino" or "concertante") against a background of the tutti group of strings called the "ripieno" (see p. 12). These *concerti grossi* were normally written in three movements. The first movement was usually in ritornello form. The middle, slow movement might be largely built on a ground bass but with changes of key, or it might be in binary form, or even in the large ternary form found in vocal arias of the period (see p. 95). The finale was usually in rondo or binary form, though another extended ritornello type of movement or a fugue was also possible.   The concerto grosso was one of the fore-runners of the symphony of Haydn, Mozart and Beethoven.

The *solo* concerto (as opposed to a concerto grosso, for a *group* of solo instruments) was similar in construction. Bach's violin concerto in E major is a well-known example. The solo part was not so important or spectacular as it became with later composers.

Concertos, like sonatas, could be styled *concerti da camera*, and *concerti da chiesa*, the latter being of a more serious nature.

Chapter Nine

Ternary Form

Ternary form is three-part form. It consists of a statement, a digression (which may be called an episode), and a restatement of the same idea. 'Charlie is my darling' is a good example of this plan in its simplest form.

But short pieces which divide into three equal parts like 'Charlie is my darling' are rather rare. There seems to be a preference for musical shape to be in multiples of two rather than three: for two- and four-bar phrases, two- and four-phrase sentences, and so on.

Four lines is the most common length for a verse of poetry, and similarly four phrases is the most common length for a short song. A A B A, as in 'All through the Night', is one of the most common plans. This is usually called ternary, (in spite of the fact that it consists of *four* phrases) because it consists of statement, digression and restatement.

A problem of terminology arises in many a minuet by Haydn, Mozart or Beethoven. Consider the well-known minuet from Mozart's symphony in E♭, K 543. Its plan is A 16 bars :‖: B 8 bars A 20 bars :‖. On paper it is in two parts, each repeated, and therefore might be called binary with the second part longer than the first. On the other hand, it consists of statement, digression and restatement, which can be called ternary; though if one listens to it performed with its repeats one hears A A B A B A, which does not seem to fit into either category. (It is customary to ignore repeats, when analysing musical form, though this means that one is judging by the eye rather than by the ear.)

Professor Tovey, the eminent musicologist, considered that the deciding factor in such cases was whether the first section was complete in itself, and ended with a finished

77

cadence in the tonic key. If it were, he considered that the essential plan was ternary, whatever the length of the succeeding B and A; whereas if A was incomplete, ending with either an imperfect cadence in the tonic, or a perfect cadence in some related key, the form as a whole fell into two parts, whatever their lengths, and was binary. Consequently he would consider the above-mentioned Mozart minuet to be binary because the first part ended in the dominant key.

Look at the scherzo of Beethoven's sonata, op. 2, no. 3. Its plan is: A 16 bars ending dominant :‖: B 23 bars. A 16 bars, changed so as to end in the tonic. Coda 9 bars :‖. Tovey would call this binary. But he would call the scherzo of op. 2, no. 2, ternary because its first part ended in the tonic. Its plan is A 8 bars ending tonic :‖: B 24 bars. A 8 bars (an exact repetition). Coda 4 bars :‖. Both, however, are A :‖: B A :‖.

It will be realised that neither of these scherzos divide visually, or aurally with repeats, into three parts; but both contain statement, digression and restatement. Some authorities, such as Macpherson and Scholes, would call both of them ternary because they each contain statement, digression and restatement. The term "extended binary" has also been used for the plan. The compromise suggested here is to call A :‖: B A :‖ "extended binary" when the first A is incomplete, and "ternary" when the first A ends with a finished cadence in the tonic key. But the plan may also be called ternary in every case; and examiners must perforce accept either term, because of these differences of terminology. Examination candidates should make it clear that they can analyse the shape of the movement, and terminology does not then matter very much.

Analyse the trios which follow these two scherzos, and decide whether you wish to say they are in binary, extended binary, or ternary form.

Notice that whereas binary form often has each part repeated thus; A :‖: B :‖ , ternary practically never has A :‖: B :‖: A :‖. It is either A :‖: B A :‖, as in most minuets and scherzos, or A :‖ B A ‖, as in 'All through the Night' and Schumann's 'Papillons' numbers 4 and 5; or

A B A as in 'Popular Song', number 9 of Schumann's 'Album for the Young'.

Extended binary or ternary form is rare in instrumental music before Haydn, though an enlarged ternary, sometimes known as *aria da capo* form was much used in vocal music by A. Scarlatti and later operatic composers such, as Handel (see p. 95).

Minuet and Trio Form

Haydn was so attracted to the minuet that he frequently included the dance as the third movement in his symphonies and chamber music, and Mozart followed suit. But a minuet, by itself, was too short to balance the other movements, so he wrote a second minuet, called a trio, as a contrast to the first, and then repeated the first minuet. (The name "trio" derived from the custom followed by Lully and other seventeenth century composers, of writing a second minuet, in an opera, for three instruments instead of for the whole orchestra.) The trio was usually in a different but related key, and well contrasted in style to the minuet.

The minuet, and the trio, considered separately, were each written in binary form, or the extended binary or ternary form described in the last section. But the second minuet (the trio) provided an episode, so that the form as a whole was an undoubted ternary. In order to avoid confusion with the use of the word "ternary" for a smaller form without subdivisions, this form has been called *extended ternary*, *compound ternary*, and *minuet and trio* form. The last of these three terms is in general use. The plan is A :‖: B (A) :‖ C :‖: D (C) :‖ A B (A) ‖. The repeats are omitted when the minuet is played for the second time.

Other dances are frequently sandwiched together in this way. Bach does it with gavottes and sarabandes in his suites; and a later composer may do it with a march or a waltz. In other words minuet and trio *form* is not confined to minuets.

The Scherzo

Haydn had already shown a disposition to produce rhythmic irregularities in the staid minuet (see the pauses in the minuet from the London Symphony). Beethoven felt the need to quicken it up and provide some humour, after his long, slow second movements. So he began to call his third movement a *scherzo*, which, in Italian, means a joke. Usually it, too, was in minuet and trio form; but there are exceptions, and the one in his piano sonata, op. 31, no. 3, is not even in triple time.

Episodical Form

This minuet and trio plan is also frequently used for pieces and movements which are not dances, and in which the sections merge into each other, instead of being in clear cut divisions, with repeats. The middle section is obviously an episode, and *episodical form* is the term in general use for this plan. It is frequently found in slow movements of sonatas. An example is the slow movement of Beethoven's piano sonata, op. 7, where the episode is preceded by a short link and merges into the return of the opening section, which latter merges, in its turn, into quite a long coda.

The Evolution of Sonata Form

Some of Bach's longer and more elaborate movements in binary form (see p. 69) show signs of developing into what is usually now called sonata form. The first half ends with a distinct cadence figure in the dominant or relative major key, while the second half ends with the same figure in the tonic. This cadence figure was further extended by his sons C. P. E. and J. C. Bach and their contemporaries, until in the hands of Haydn it emerged as a definite second subject.

Also the second part of such a highly developed binary movement was considerably longer than the first, and began by modulating freely into other related keys. This modulatory part later became the development section of sonata form.

After this tonal digression it began to be felt that a return to the opening bars in the *tonic* key was necessary, and this marks what we now call the recapitulation. In other words, the second part of the binary movement split up into the development and recapitulation of sonata form.

It will thus be seen that sonata form, which seems to us today to be clearly in three parts, grew from the binary form of Bach's day. It evolved very gradually, and many varieties of growth can be seen in the period between J. S. Bach and Haydn, though music of this experimental period is not often heard today. By the time of Haydn and Mozart the form had emerged in its broad outlines as a plan on which the most highly developed movements were to be based for the next hundred years or so. The contrast between the two subjects (or groups of subjects) became more marked, as sonata form became progressively more dramatic in the hands of Beethoven. Such contrasts within a movement were unknown in the time of Bach.

Sonata Form

The general plan of sonata form is as follows:—

Exposition	Development	Recapitulation
First subject in tonic; usually rhythmical, short and assertive.	The composer develops any material from the exposition in any way he likes, and in any key. He may also introduce new material, i.e. an episode.	*First subject*, tonic, as before.
Transition, leading to the key and mood of		*Transition*, modified so as to lead to
Second subject, usually in dominant or relative major; melodious, and often in several sections.		*Second subject*, tonic.
Codetta, to round off the exposition.		*Codetta*, as before, but in tonic.

A slow introduction, or a coda may be added.

"Sonata form" and "first movement form" are both misleading titles, but one or other is always used for this plan. It should be realised that the form is not the form of a whole sonata, but merely of one movement of it; also that it is not

6

confined either to first movements or sonatas. It is often found in second and last movements, and in symphonies, concertos, all kinds of chamber music, and even in one-movement forms, such as overture. In fact, for a hundred years composers used it as the chief vehicle for their finest large-scale conceptions. It not only has great dramatic possibilities but also gives great freedom. The second-rate composers may conform to a regular plan, but there is nearly always something "irregular" or unexpected in the works of the greatest composers. Do not feel that because Haydn uses the same theme for first and second subjects, or Mozart introduces his second subject before the first in the recapitulation that they are doing something wrong! The test is whether the movement hangs together satisfactorily as a whole, and a composer like Beethoven can make all sorts of irregularities sound convincing.

This form can be studied in relation to any of the many examples available. A movement by Haydn or Mozart will be short and easy to follow, though even these composers may have a number of themes in the second subject group, and Haydn often makes changes in the recapitulation. In addition to a repeat of the exposition, the development and recapitulation may be repeated together too, thus showing that the composer is thinking of the movement as being an enlargement of binary form with the two sections repeated.

Beethoven still repeats the exposition, but his movements are usually longer, more dramatic and more of an organic whole. The transition may be new material or may grow out of the first subject, but it will not be an obvious join. In some cases, Beethoven experiments with an unusual key for the second subject—for example, the second subject of the first movement of the 'Waldstein' sonata is in the mediant major. His developments are longer and full of unexpected touches and unusual modulations, while his codas are sometimes so long and so full of further development as almost to constitute a fourth section.

Schubert and Brahms often write melodious tunes even for the first subjects; and Brahms, like Beethoven, writes fine development sections. At times they both end this section with a long dominant pedal, over which is built an exciting climax leading into the recapitulation—for example the first movement of Beethoven's 'Pathétique' and 'Waldstein' sonatas. In the first movement of Brahms's D minor violin sonata the whole of the development section is built on a pedal.

Modified Sonata Form

Sonata form is frequently used for a quick first or last movement. If it is used for a slow movement there is a danger of it becoming too long. In such cases the composer sometimes leaves out the development section, perhaps having a short link between exposition and recapitulation. This plan is usually called modified or abridged sonata form. It will be found in the slow movement of Beethoven's piano sonata, op. 2, no. 3. It is also often used for overtures, as in Mozart's overture to the 'Marriage of Figaro'.

Sonata Rondo Form

The plan of sonata rondo form is as follows:

Exposition	Middle Section	Recapitulation
First subject in tonic.	Usually an episode in another related key; but it may contain some development.	*First subject* in tonic.
Transition.		*Transition* (modified).
Second subject, usually in dominant or relative major.		*Second subject*, in tonic.
Transition.		*Transition* (modified).
First subject in tonic.		*First subject* in tonic (may be considerably shortened, or may merge into a coda).

It is a combination of the old rondo form, with its clearly defined sections and often dance-like rhythm, and the more organic, unified sonata form. It usually has the gay dance-like quality of the rondo, but it has links and transitions joining the sections. The second theme occurs twice, so it is called a second subject instead of an episode.

The form divides into three main sections, like sonata form, but the exposition and recapitulation end with a return or at least a reference to the first subject, and the middle section is usually an episode, though it may consist partly or even entirely of development.

Beethoven frequently uses this form for his last movements —for example, the piano sonatas op. 2, no. 2; op. 2, no. 3; and op. 7.

Movements are sometimes found which seem to be such a mixture of sonata and sonata rondo that it is possible to say they are in either form. The last movement of Beethoven's eighth symphony is a case in point. And occasionally a movement will be called a rondo by the composer, though it is not in rondo form at all! But it probably has a recurring, rondo-like theme.

Chapter Ten

The Sonata

The sonata of Corelli and Bach gradually merged into that of Haydn, Mozart and Beethoven, and, in so doing, the term began to have a much more exact meaning. It became applied to a work written for not more than two instruments, containing at least two, and usually three or four contrasted movements. The first movement was usually quick and in sonata form; the second was slow, and frequently in episodical, variation or modified sonata form; the third (if present) was a minuet or a scherzo with a trio; and the finale was usually quick and gay, and probably in rondo, sonata, or sonata rondo form. The third movement was the only relic of the dances of the suite.

The first and last movements were always in the tonic key, and so, usually, was the minuet or scherzo. But the second movement changed to some related key other than the dominant or relative major, the complementary key of the first movement, and was often on the flat side of the tonic. This change of key seems to us, today, to be a welcome departure from the fixed tonality of the suite.

Many sonatas will be found that do not keep to the above-mentioned scheme. Beethoven's 'Moonlight' sonata, which begins with a slow movement, was labelled by him 'sonata quasi una fantasia'. First movements in variation form, and fugal-type finales are other possibilities.

Chamber Music

Chamber music is music for a room (da camera), in contrast to a theatre or a church (da chiesa). The term originally included vocal as well as instrumental music, and music for a small orchestra. Cantatas, sonatas, and concertos "da camera" were all species of chamber music.

Gradually the term was narrowed down to apply to instrumental music for groups of solo performers. But even as late as Haydn, the distinction between chamber and orchestral music was not as clearly defined as it is today. We are not sure whether some of his very early string works were intended for quartet or small orchestra.

The fundamental difference between chamber music of the Corelli-Bach period and that of Haydn and later composers, is that the continuo was an essential feature of all chamber works in the former period, while the later composers ceased to use it. Each instrument became equally important, and no background was required.

The term sonata is applied to works for one or two instruments, trio for three, quartet for four, etc. Notice that the word trio has three meanings: (a) a group of three performers, whether vocal or instrumental; (b) a sonata for three instruments; (c) a dance movement providing an episode to a minuet or scherzo or similar movement. A string trio is usually for violin, viola and 'cello, while a piano trio is for piano, violin and 'cello.

A string quartet is written for two violins, viola and 'cello. Piano quartets are for piano, violin, viola and 'cello, and piano quintets add a second violin. There are also quartets for a wind instrument, such as an oboe or clarinet, with strings, and works for wind instruments alone. String sextets are for two violins, two violas, and two 'cellos. Chamber music literature includes music for all sorts of combinations, and practically all these works are built on the sonata plan.

The Overture

The overture came into existence in the seventeenth century, as an orchestral introduction to an opera or an oratorio.

Lully (1632–1687) popularised the *French overture*, consisting of a slow introduction in a dotted rhythm, followed by a quick fugato. Sometimes this was followed by a dance movement or two. This plan was much used by Bach and Handel. The overture to Handel's 'Messiah' has a slow ♩.♪ introduction, followed by a fugue; while his 'Samson' overture includes a charming minuet after the fugue.

A French overture followed by a series of dances became, in effect, a suite, and some suites of this period were called overtures.

The *Italian overture*, popularised by A. Scarlatti (1660–1725), consisted of three movements, quick, slow, quick. Another name for it was *sinfonia avanti l'opera*. Such works were occasionally performed in a concert hall, without the opera, and were thus the forerunners of the symphony.

During the eighteenth century the overture was reduced to one movement, usually in the new sonata or modified sonata form. Sometimes themes from the opera were used in the overture, as, for example, with Weber and Wagner.

Beethoven wrote overtures such as 'Egmont' and 'Coriolanus', which were preludes to plays, as did also Schubert with his 'Rosamunde'.

Overtures originally written as preludes to operas and plays began to be played by themselves at the beginning of a concert, and it was but a step from this to the *concert overture*, which, though usually based on a story (programme music), was not a prelude to a larger work. Such works are Mendelssohn's 'A Midsummer Night's Dream' and 'Fingal's Cave', Brahms's 'Academic Festival', and Elgar's 'Cockaigne' and 'In the South'. Most of these works are still in a loose kind of sonata form.

The Symphony

This term, like sonata, originally had a wide connotation. It literally means "sounding together". The instrumental introduction to a song was, at one time, called the opening symphony. The 'Pastoral Symphony' in Handel's 'Messiah' is so called in contrast to the vocal numbers. Gradually the term was applied to an orchestral piece, such as the *sinfonia avanti l'opera* mentioned above, and then to a completely separate work. The form and style grew partly from the Italian overture and partly from the concerto grosso.

With the development of sonata form it became, in effect, a sonata for orchestra. It had a slow introduction more often than did a sonata, and was almost invariably in four movements, while the sonata was often in three.

Works in several movements are sometimes called *cyclic* forms. At first the movements were completely separate. But Beethoven has a wonderful link between the third and fourth movements of his fifth symphony, and he quotes themes from the earlier movements in the finale of his 'Choral' symphony. Schumann links the movements together in his fourth symphony and uses the same themes in different movements. The recurrence, and sometimes the metamorphosis of themes in different movements became more general in later symphonies, as for example in Tschaikowsky's E minor symphony, Dvořák's 'New World', and Franck's symphony in D minor. The term 'cyclic' is reserved by some authorities for those works in which the same theme occurs in more than one movement. Sometimes, too, a symphony was linked with a story, as in Berlioz's 'Symphonie Fantastique'. In this work he uses one theme, which he calls "L'idée fixe", to represent the heroine, and it undergoes various transformations in the different movements, rather like the *Leitmotiv* which Wagner later used in his operas (see p. 95).

Brahms was the greatest symphonic composer in the second half of the nineteenth century, and composers such as Sibelius, Elgar, Vaughan Williams and Walton have continued to write symphonies in the twentieth century, though they have become progressively more free in form and style.

The Concerto

The old types of solo concerto and concerto grosso died out with Bach and with the disuse of the continuo. The new type adopted the form of the new sonata, but it was almost invariably in three movements, omitting the third, the dance, movement.

The first movement of a concerto by Mozart usually began with an opening tutti, rather like the opening ritornello of the concerto grosso, in which the main themes of the movement were stated. This corresponded to the exposition of sonata form, except that the second subject usually appeared in the tonic key. The soloist then entered with decorated versions of the themes, accompanied by the orchestra, but with the second subject now in the usual related key. This was rather like the repetition of the exposition in sonata form, but with the repeat written out because of the varied treatment provided by the entry of the soloist.

Another tutti led into the development section, and yet another into the recapitulation. Towards the end of the movement another tutti led to a pause on a cadential six-four (Ic), which was a signal for the soloist to improvise a cadenza, making further use of the themes as his fancy dictated. Finally he would return to the Ic previously stated by the orchestra, and resolve it on to V, probably with a series of trills, which was a signal for the orchestra to re-enter for the coda.

This plan underwent several modifications as time went on. Sometimes the soloist began with an introductory fanfare; sometimes soloist and orchestra entered together and the repeated exposition was dispensed with. But Brahms uses a preliminary orchestral exposition in all his concertos.

The cadenza, too, underwent modification. Probably few soloists were capable of improvising a really good cadenza (even if they had prepared it beforehand!), and later composers began to write out their own cadenzas.

Short cadenzas sometimes occurred in other movements, and in general the later concerto became much more a display of virtuosity on the part of the soloist than the eighteenth-century concerto had been. But in the best examples the orchestral part is far more than a mere accompaniment.

Although most post-Mozartian concertos are for a solo

instrument there are a few double and triple concertos, including a magnificent one by Brahms for violin and 'cello.

Absolute and Programme Music

The earliest written music was entirely vocal, and so was always linked to a verbal meaning. With the rise of instrumental music two types came into being—*absolute* and *programme*. Absolute, or abstract music is music which is complete in itself, which depends for its beauty upon its musical qualities, its melody, harmony, rhythm, form, dynamics and tone colour. Programme music is music which is based on something extraneous to music, such as a poem, a story, a mood, a picture, or nature. The term was first used by Liszt, but the idea is as old as instrumental music itself, for even Byrd wrote a piece called 'The March before the Battle'. Couperin gave his harpsichord pieces titles as mentioned on p. 71, Handel depicted the plagues in 'Israel in Egypt', and even Beethoven wrote a 'Battle Symphony'.

Programme music really came into its own in the nineteenth century, however, with the development of "romantic" music, the growing literary interests of many composers, and the possibilities inherent in the variety of tone colour of the ever growing orchestral resources. Many programmatic orchestral pieces were written (see "symphonic poem," p. 90), and the impressionists (see p. 183) also gave titles to their compositions.

The Symphonic Poem   or Tone Poem.

This term was first used by Liszt (1811–1886). Another name for it is "tone poem". It is a large orchestral work, generally in one movement, which depends upon an external "programme" for its musical ideas and shape, though it is frequently in a very loose kind of sonata form. Most of Liszt's symphonic poems have not lived, but Richard Strauss (1864–1949) developed the medium and his 'Till Eulenspiegel' and 'Ein Heldenleben' are two fine examples. Smetana wrote six tone poems called 'My Fatherland'; and 'Finlandia' and 'The Swan of Tuonela' by Sibelius are also well known. It is customary in symphonic poems, as in all programme music, to associate a theme with a person or an idea, and to allow it to develop in accordance with the story.

Chapter Eleven

Early Vocal Music

The earliest written music was entirely vocal. There is a brief account of plainsong and the forms arising from it, and of motets, madrigals, ayres and ballets in Chapter Seven.

The Mass

The mass is the chief service of the Roman Catholic Church, and roughly corresponds to the celebration of the Eucharist or Holy Communion in the Anglican Church. "High Mass" is a sung mass, and composers have written settings to it from the earliest times.

Certain parts of the mass vary according to the time of the church year, and these are usually sung to their traditional plainsong tunes. The "Ordinary" is the part of the mass which does not vary. Its musical sections consist of the *Kyrie, Gloria, Credo, Sanctus*, and *Agnus Dei*. *Kyrie Eleison* is Greek, the rest is Latin. At first these sections, too, were in plainsong, and plainsong is still in regular use on ordinary occasions and in smaller churches. But gradually a more elaborate contrapuntal style began to be used for special occasions, so that these sections were not unlike a series of motets. This style of unaccompanied vocal writing culminated in the magnificent masses of Palestrina, written at the end of the sixteenth century. A *Requiem* is a mass for the dead. Brahms's German Requiem is not a mass; nor, liturgically speaking, is Delius's 'Mass of Life'. Neither of them uses the words of the liturgy.

Folk Songs and Ballads

At the same time as early vocal music was being written by church and secular musicians, the simpler folk made

up their own folk songs. They were originally for unaccompanied solo voice and were not written down, so that, in the
course of passing from singer to singer, they underwent frequent changes, and many variants of the same folksong may
be in existence today.

They were divided into verses, with the same tune for
each verse (strophic); and they naturally had many of the
characteristics of the written music of the period, such as
being based on the old modes and using a free rhythm like
plainsong.

Each country had its own characteristic types, but in the
course of time the songs tended to become modernised and
to lose their special characteristics. Many were written
down round about 1900, when, owing to the spread of
urbanisation, they were just about to die out. Composers
such as Bartok in Hungary, and Vaughan Williams in
England, have made use of folk song in their compositions.

The *Ballad* was a poem telling a story in verses. In
English it usually had four lines of $8+6+8+6$ syllables,
which is the same as the "common metre" of a hymn tune.
It was set to a strophic tune, and as time went on, began to
be written down, and sold to the public on "ballad sheets".
Ballads were popular in Elizabethan days, and there are
several references to them in Shakespeare's plays. Later
again, they began to have a simple accompaniment, but it
was entirely subordinate to the tune. Sometimes an
occasional verse was set to a different tune, but the style was
still simple and unsophisticated. Ballads were very popular
in drawing-rooms of the Victorian era.

Sea-shanties and other working songs such as milking
croons, carols and negro spirituals are all varieties of folk
song.

Opera

The birth of opera took place round about 1600 (see
p. 108). Plays with music had been performed before this
date, sometimes with the actors miming or speaking on the
stage while singers sang madrigals behind the stage.

But this new kind of work, opera, largely consisted of *recitative*. In this, individual actors on the stage sang with the free rhythm and inflexions of speech. They were accompanied by a harpsichord, which played occasional punctuating chords from figured bass, with the lower strings playing the bass line at the same time. (See "continuo", p. 8). *Coloratura* passages were also written for the singers. These were highly decorative runs and cadenzas, supposed to give "colour" to the words, but in reality serving to show off the vocal abilities of the singer. There were occasional choruses, too, but they were more homophonic in style than the madrigal. A varied collection of orchestral instruments were used for accompaniment and for occasional orchestral interludes. Monteverdi's operas were of this type.

Gradually, during the seventeenth century, two types of recitative were evolved. They were:

(i) *Recitativo Secco* (dry recitative) This was unaccompanied except for the harpsichord punctuations. It moved nearly as quickly as speech, and was therefore particularly suitable for explanatory passages requiring speed.

(ii) *Recitativo stromentato*, or *accompagnato* (accompanied recitative). This was accompanied by the orchestra, so the singer's rhythm could not be free, as he had to keep in time with the orchestra. It was more tuneful than *recitativo secco*, but still moved quite quickly, without any repetitions of words. It was more dramatic than *secco*.

Well-known examples of these two types are 'There were Shepherds abiding in the Fields', which is *secco*, followed by 'And suddenly there was with the Angels', which is *stromentato*, from Handel's 'Messiah'.

Recitativo stromentato is half way between *recitativo secco* and the *aria* or air; and another name for it is *arioso*, that is, aria-like. Bach often wrote arioso passages, which were almost like a little aria. Wagner's operatic style was a continuous arioso, for he had no use either for the *recitativo secco* or the formal aria. But he used a much more powerful and important orchestral accompaniment than the early operatic composers had done.

The Operatic Aria

As said above, the earliest operas consisted largely of recitative. But gradually more melodious passages began to creep in, particularly at the more static moments of the story when there was an opportunity for the singer to soliloquise, and the operatic aria (air) was born. Monteverdi produced some of the first examples, and gradually the style and form became standardised until, by the time of Alessandro Scarlatti (1660–1725), it had become a fixed convention.

This *aria da capo* form consisted of an instrumental introduction followed by a first vocal section beginning and ending in the tonic. After another instrumental ritornello there followed a second vocal section in a contrasted style and key, ending with the letters D.C. (da capo). This meant that the whole of the first section had to be repeated, which, for us today, often seems wearisome. But the singer was free to add any embellishments such as runs and trills that he or she wished in this *da capo*, and the Italians loved this opportunity for vocal display.

This large-scale ternary form was much used in opera and oratorio in the seventeenth and eighteenth centuries. Handel's 'Where'er you walk' is an example of it.

But all arias were not in this form. Bach frequently used the ritornello form described on p. 74 in his vocal works. Gluck did not use the *da capo* aria at all, as he felt that it interrupted the drama too much; and the arias of the nineteenth-century operatic composers were much freer in form. Composers sometimes used the word "scena" for a long vocal solo in which recitatives and arias alternated.

Wagner's operas and those of many other later operatic composers did not divide into separate "numbers", but used a free arioso style almost throughout. Wagner used *Leitmotive* to represent certain persons or ideas and to bind together the continuous musical texture. He preferred to call his works "music dramas" rather than "operas".

Concerted Operatic Numbers

The earliest operas were mainly for a group of solo singers. But gradually "ensembles" of soloists were included. There are several in Mozart's 'Marriage of Figaro', and one of the most famous is the quintet in Act III of Wagner's 'Mastersingers'.

The chorus began to be used more, too. Verdi's 'Aida' is an opera which makes great use of the chorus.

Mozart was one of the first composers to write an extended "finale" at the end of an act, in which a series of short solos, ensembles, and sometimes choruses, were used. A particularly fine example is the finale to Act I of 'The Magic Flute'.

The Ballet

The ballet was also a feature of longer and more elaborate operas. It was largely developed in seventeenth-century France, at the court of Louis XIV. Gavottes, minuets and bourrées were popular, as well as dances which told a story. Sometimes the ballet was a complete entertainment in itself, though it might contain a little singing; sometimes it was part of an opera. Lully (1632–1687) wrote many ballets of both kinds.

In the eighteenth and nineteenth centuries Paris remained the chief centre of the ballet, but Russian ballet became more important during this time. Under the direction of the impresario Diaghileff (1872–1929) it became more dramatic and made greater use of male dancers. The music of many ballets has been turned into orchestral suites.

Oratorio

Oratorio took its name from St Philip Neri's oratory in Rome, where, at the beginning of the seventeenth century, the first oratorios were performed. They were very similar to the operas written at this period, except that they were on a sacred subject and were performed by the College of

Oratorians in church. Originally they had scenery, costumes and action, as had opera, and were a growth from the mystery and miracle plays of the middle ages, the main difference being that every word was sung.

Gradually the oratorios ceased to be acted, though they were performed in concert halls and theatres as well as in churches. They degenerated into a musical entertainment, which, apart from the subject, was identical with opera. They consisted of recitatives, arias and choruses, with an orchestral accompaniment, and provided plenty of opportunity for vocal display. Handel turned to oratorio from opera comparatively late in life, and, with the exception of the 'Messiah', the style of the two types of works is indistinguishable. Oratorio has been very popular in England ever since the days of Handel.

The Chorale

"Choral" is the German word for a hymn tune, and it is usually translated into English as "chorale". The chorale grew from the plainsong of the Roman Catholic church, but Luther (1483–1546), the great reformer, wished the congregation to take a larger part in the church service, so the German language was used instead of Latin, and simple hymns were included which the congregation could sing. Luther wrote the words of many of these hymns himself, and even a few of the tunes. At first the melody was in the tenor, but by Bach's day it had moved to the treble. Bach wrote a few original chorales, but his main contribution was reharmonising many of the traditional old ones, and he sometimes wrote several harmonisations of the same tune.

The chorale had a great influence on German music. The church was the centre of musical life in Bach's day, and everyone knew the chorale tunes. So it was natural that organ pieces, called *chorale preludes*, should be built on chorale tunes, and that chorales should form part of cantatas and oratorios. 'Now thank we all our God', 'A safe Stronghold', 'Wake, O Wake, for Night is Flying', and 'O sacred Head, sore Wounded', are four very well-known chorales.

7

Cantata

A cantata is a poem or a story set to vocal music. It may consist of solos, concerted numbers such as duets and trios, choruses, or a mixture of all three. It is usually accompanied by an orchestra, and it may be sacred or secular. It is often like a short opera or oratorio but intended for performance without scenery or action. As with the sonata, there were two forms originally, *cantata da camera*, and *cantata da chiesa*, and their development followed on the same lines as that of opera and oratorio.

Bach was the greatest writer of cantatas. He wrote five complete sets for the ecclesiastical year, and 200 of these are still extant. Most of them contain at least one setting of a chorale, in addition to solos and duets. Frequently they began with an elaborate chorale setting, in which each line of a slow moving chorale was treated in turn by quicker contrapuntal imitations; and they frequently ended with a simple four-part harmonic setting, in which the congregation could join. 'Sleepers Wake' is a fine example. The 'Christmas Oratorio' really consists of six cantatas intended for performance on six different days of the Christmas festival.

Passion Music

Plays enacting the Passion of Christ were acted in churches during the Middle Ages, and music was sometimes added to them. It was also the custom of priests to recite the story of the Passion in church in Holy Week, and this, too, was later set to music. A tenor always took the part of the Narrator or *Historicus*, a bass sang the part of Christ, and choruses were used either to represent the crowds in the bible story, or to comment on the story, or both. At first the words were in Latin, but, after the reformation, they were translated into the vernacular. Schütz (1585–1672) wrote some fine settings in German, but the best known are those by Bach. It is not certain whether he wrote three, four or five passions, but only the St Matthew, the St

John and a part of the St Mark are now extant. The St Matthew is the largest and greatest. It contains a number of chorales, some of which were probably sung by the congregation. The 'Passion Chorale' occurs no less than five times, in five different keys and harmonised in four different ways. The words of Christ are always accompanied by strings, in contrast to the *secco* recitative of the rest, and give almost the effect of a halo.

The Lied or Art Song

The development of instruments in the sixteenth century resulted in the growth of solo songs with an instrumental accompaniment, as distinct from the unsophisticated unaccompanied folk-song. Songs with lute accompaniment rapidly became popular throughout Europe, and Dowland wrote some lovely ones in England, such as 'Flow not so fast, ye fountains'.

The German word for song is "Lied", and Schubert is generally considered to be the first great writer of *Lieder*, or art songs, with piano accompaniment. In his songs the piano part is as important as the voice part, and the two together express the meaning of the words, sometimes very dramatically. 'The Erl King' is an outstanding example.

In some of the simplest of his songs he treats the words strophically, as in 'Who is Sylvia'. But more often he composes the song in one continuous whole (called *durchcomponirt* in German), and he lets the words decide the shape of the music, so that the formal construction is very free. This is quite different from the conventional operatic aria, with its verbal repetitions and its standard design. "Whither" well repays analysis, but it cannot be labelled as being in any particular form.

Other great German Lieder writers were Schumann, Brahms, Wolf and Richard Strauss. Debussy and Ravel have written art songs in France, and England possesses some fine twentieth-century song writers, including Frank Bridge, John Ireland, Arnold Bax, Peter Warlock, Armstrong Gibbs, Gerald Finzi, Vaughan Williams and Benjamin Britten.

PART III

MUSICAL HISTORY

Chapter Twelve

The Music of Primitive Peoples

It is always hard for anyone to imagine a world completely different from the one in which he has been brought up. All of us in Europe today take it for granted that we shall be surrounded by music of all kinds: at school, in church, in the cinema, on radio and television in the home; music on all kinds of instruments, using melody and harmony, and complicated rhythms and musical forms. Yet it has taken many centuries for all these aspects of music to be built up, and it is worth while trying to get an imaginative picture of earlier civilisations, and realising what sort of music surrounded the lives of people who lived in those times. For always there was music, no matter how primitive the people, and it has always taken a large part in people's lives, however strange some of it may seem to us today.

Television and the cinema have made most of us acquainted with the music making of primitive peoples, as seen and heard on the films which explorers have brought back from Africa or aboriginal Australia. The music may seem queer to us. It is not based on our scales, does not use our harmonies or our kinds of musical instruments, and it seems to us to be very monotonous, as it repeats the same phrase over and over again. But obviously it gives great pleasure to the people who make it, just as ours does to us in Europe. There must have been a time when music similar to this was the only kind to be heard in the world.

The Music of Classical Greece

Greece is considered to be the cradle of our European civilisation. We know that the classical Greeks valued music very highly. Plato considered that music and gymnastics were the two essentials in education, though both these terms covered very much more than they do today. But we do not really know what their music sounded like. We know that they had various forms of scales, but the size of their intervals was not the same as ours, so that any attempt to reproduce their music sounds out of tune to us. Men sang an octave below women and boys, just as they do today; but apart from that, their music was entirely melodic. It was very much linked up with verse, as, for example, in the choruses to the Greek plays, which may have sounded rather like our modern choral speech. Pipes and lyres often accompanied the voice, either in unison with the singer or on a drone.

Early Music of the Christian Church. Plainsong

The earliest music of the Christian Church borrowed much from the Greeks and from the Jews, who have always been a music-loving people. Singing was a part of church worship from the very beginning. St Ambrose, bishop of Milan, made a collection of tunes in the fourth century, and in the sixth century the great pope, St Gregory, collected the large body of plainsong which is known as Gregorian plainchant, and is still sung in churches today.

But again our imagination has to be exercised when we realise that, before the ninth century, A.D., no one had thought of producing a chord. Imagine a world without "harmony" of any kind!

The Development of Polyphonic Music up to 1550

Some time during the ninth century the most important event in the whole of European musical history happened

—church musicians began to sing in chords. Nature has created women and children with high and low voices, and men with high and low voices about an octave below those of women and children. A tune that suits the range of a treble voice will fit an alto voice if it is sung a fourth of fifth lower, while tenor and bass voices will find it convenient to sing an octave below the treble and alto. And so the boys and men in church choirs began to sing in *organum*, an example of which is quoted on p. 63. Probably they did not realise what a wonderful new thing they were doing, and what far-reaching consequences it was going to have. But, once having heard parallel fourths, fifths and octaves, the way was open to experiment with other intervals, and with movement that was not always parallel.

And so, for several hundred years, the monks experimented with musical composition, gradually evolving rules, and also devising a notation in which to write down their music. It is a fascinating story, but it would take too long to tell here.

This early music was almost entirely vocal, for instruments were still too primitive to be used for serious music. But sometimes the monks wrote secular music, in addition to music for the church. For example, a monk from Reading Abbey, called John of Fornsete, wrote 'Sumer is i-cumen in' round about 1240. You may know it, as it is still sung today.

The monks had worked out a system of scales called modes. Our major mode was one of them, but they liked this the least! The others can be found by playing a scale on the white notes of the piano, starting on each note in turn. For example, the mode from D to D is called Dorian, and the mode from A to A Aeolian. Music based on these modes sounds strange to us today, but they were in use right through the days of Queen Elizabeth I, and only began to die out with the development of opera in the seventeenth century.

As a result of the Renaissance and the spread of learning and education throughout Europe, music began to widen its bounds. Other people, beside monks, began to compose and perform music; and secular music, mainly intended for the homes of the wealthier classes and the aristocracy, developed rapidly. Then, too, there was the unwritten folk-music sung by the people of every country, which is referred to on p. 92. By about 1550 the stage is set for us to begin the study of individual composers and of music which we can understand and enjoy today.

Chapter Thirteen

Palestrina

Some of the most beautiful church music of all time was written in the second half of the sixteenth century. There were great composers in many European countries, but perhaps the greatest of them all was the Italian Palestrina (1525–1594). He took his name from the small town near Rome in which he was born. He was a choir boy in a church in Rome, and later became the organist and choir-master of the cathedral of his home town. When he was 25 the Bishop of Palestrina was made pope, and, realising his choirmaster's genius, he appointed him to be choir-master at the Sistine Chapel. At 30 he was made a member of the papal choir, though his appointment was short-lived, as he was married, and a new pope refused to allow married men in his choir. However, Palestrina spent the rest of his life in Rome, most of the time in the service of the church. Gradually he became known as Rome's greatest composer.

The famous Council of Trent met in 1562 and advised that church music should be "purged of all sensual and impure elements, all secular forms and unedifying language". Palestrina's music kept to the spirit of this recommendation, and it has a sublime beauty which makes it a perfect expression of religious feeling. There is a great deal of smooth, stepwise movement, and although each melodic part is tuneful in itself, it blends with the others to make a perfect whole. His music was entirely vocal, and was based on the old modes. The words were always in Latin.

Palestrina wrote 93 masses, and about 600 motets and other liturgical music. His best-known work is the 'Missa Papae Marcelli' which was dedicated to a pope who had reigned for three weeks when Palestrina was 30 and who had asked for his singers to perform "in a suitable manner, with properly modulated voices, so that everything could be both heard and properly understood". Palestrina took three or four years to write the work, and dedicated it to his memory.

English Church Music in Tudor Times

Apart from the works of Palestrina, most of the music of this period that you are likely to hear is English. English music in the days of Queen Elizabeth I was second to none, and we can be very proud of our heritage.

Tye (*c.* 1500–*c.* 1573) and *Tallis* (*c.* 1505–1585) were two great composers who wrote church music before the Reformation. Tye was choirmaster at Ely cathedral and Tallis was the organist of Waltham Abbey. They wrote masses and motets and other music for the Roman Catholic church service. But they, like all other church musicians, were affected by the Reformation. The monasteries had been the chief seats of musical learning, so they were naturally affected by their closure. Tallis lost his post on the dissolution of Waltham Abbey, but he later became a Gentleman of the Chapel Royal of King Henry VIII. This Chapel was the religious establishment of the Sovereign, members of which always travelled with him to perform the daily service. It consisted of "Gentlemen" singers, and of boys who were known as the "Children of the Chapel". They wore a brilliant uniform, rather like that of the Yeomen of the Guard. Many other famous musicians, such as Purcell and Sullivan, have been Children or Gentlemen of the Chapel, and it still sings twice on Sundays in St James's Palace, a building which was built by Henry VIII.

The Tudors were a musical family, and Henry VIII was a composer, in addition to being a patron of the art. The Reformation brought political rather than theological changes in his reign, and Tye was able to continue as organist at Ely. But greater changes took place when Edward VI came to the throne. He issued the first English prayer book in 1549, and composers had then to begin writing church music with English rather than Latin words, while musical services which had been previously written in Latin could no longer be used, unless they were rewritten to English words. Tallis was among the first composers to write in English, and he has been called "the Father of English Cathedral music". Tye also wrote for the reformed church, in a simple tuneful style, and has been called "the Father of the anthem". The anthem was similar to the motet, but with English instead of Latin words.

Greater than either Tye or Tallis was *William Byrd* (1543–1623). He lived a generation later, through the reign of Queen Elizabeth and on into Stuart days. Yet he remained a convinced Catholic, and wrote much church music with Latin words. He and his wife and family were indicted several times for not attending their parish church, and on one occasion his house was searched, but he suffered no real persecution, and he was allowed to retain his appointment as joint organist with Tallis of the Chapel Royal, probably because he was so highly esteemed as a musician. He wrote some fine masses in Latin, in addition to music with English words for the Protestant church, such as his 'Great Service'. There had been so many recent changes in religion, and perhaps he always hoped that England would become Roman Catholic again.

In 1575 Byrd and Tallis obtained a monopoly from Queen Elizabeth to be the sole music printers and publishers in England, and they jointly composed a set of motets called 'Cantiones Sacrae', dedicated to the Queen in that year. Byrd was a prolific composer and he wrote many madrigals and a good deal of music for the viols and virginals. But he was a deeply serious and religious man, and his church music is perhaps his greatest contribution to posterity.

Secular Music in Tudor Times

Church music was not the only kind that flourished in this period. So many composers wrote madrigals (see p. 63) that it is only possible to name a few, such as *Morley*, *Weelkes*, *Wilbye*, *Gibbons* and *Byrd*. Morley edited a famous collection by a number of composers called 'The Triumphs of Oriana'. It used to be thought they were dedicated to Queen Elizabeth; and each one praised her with words such as "Long live fair Oriana". But she died just before they were published. However, some authorities now say that they were intended for Anne of Denmark, and not for Elizabeth at all. Madrigal singing was a very popular pursuit in the homes of the educated. Each singer was expected to read his or her part at sight. They often sat round a table, each with his own part in front of him. No bar lines were used, and the music was still based on the old church modes.

Towards the end of Elizabeth's reign a new variety of music making began to come to the fore, that of solo singing to a lute accompaniment. *Dowland* became known as the greatest composer and finest performer of these "ayres" and he can be considered the chief pioneer in the development of the art song (see p. 99). For the first time the "top" part became more important than the others, and the lute provided a real accompaniment. Compare this with a madrigal, in which all the voices are equally important.

In Tudor times the first instrumental music began to be written. In addition to the lute, which was mainly used to accompany singers, many fantasies were written for consorts of viols (see p. 1). The virginal was also popular. *John Bull* wrote a famous show-piece for it called 'The King's Hunt'; *Giles Farnaby* wrote some delightful little pieces; and *Byrd* wrote many dances and sets of variations for keyboard instruments.

Chapter Fourteen

The Birth and Growth of Opera in the Seventeenth Century

The seventeenth century was an experimental period in music: the foundations of our modern music were laid at that time. Monteverdi, Lully, Corelli, Purcell, A. Scarlatti and Couperin are the greatest musicians of the century.

The birth of opera, round about 1600, was the root cause of all the musical changes that were to occur in the century. There had been religious plays with music from the tenth century, and towards the end of the Middle Ages secular plays began to develop. There were also entertainments for special occasions, like masques. But opera, as we know it today, resulted from the meetings of a group of poets and musicians in a nobleman's house in Florence. Their interest in Ancient Greece had been aroused by the Renaissance, and their intention was to revive Greek drama. But they knew even less about it than we do today, and what they inadvertently produced was a new art, "opera in musica", or "opera" for short.

They wished to produce a dramatic work, and they realised that polyphonic madrigals were not suitable for the purpose. So they invented *recitative* (see p. 94), which gave a solo singer on the stage the chance to declaim the words with a dramatic effect. It required an accompaniment; but the addition of other voices, as in the madrigal, would have prevented the solo voice from standing out sufficiently. So they used a harpsichord accompaniment, which had quite a different sound, and its function was merely to accompany the voice in simple block chords. These were indicated by figuring, and the harpsichordist was free to arrange the chords as he pleased. This "monodic" style of writing, in which one part was pre-eminent and the rest merely an accompaniment, was a complete revolution from the polyphonic style of Palestrina and the madrigalists, in which all the parts were equally important, and it had far-reaching effects on the future history of the art of music, as will be seen later.

Peri and *Caccini* were two of the earliest opera composers, and they each wrote a setting of the story of Orpheus in 1600. They used recitative most of the time, but there were occasionally more ornate passages of *coloratura*, and a few simple instrumental interludes.

The new art spread rapidly throughout Italy, and further developments were made. The more formal aria (see p. 95) began to be used, in addition to recitative, and the number of instruments used for various effects grew. *Monteverdi* (1567–1643) was the first great operatic composer, and he, too, wrote a setting of Orpheus, in 1608. He had a strong dramatic sense, and he loved experimenting with harmonic colour and with the tone qualities of different instruments. He was one of the first composers to use discords without preparation, and to use the tremolo (rapid repeated notes) on the violins, and these devices excited audiences very much. He used quite a large orchestra, a miscellaneous collection of instruments of the day, such as lutes, viols, violins, harps, small organs, cornetti (a kind of recorder with a cup mouth-piece), and trumpets. The recitatives were still frequently accompanied by the harpsichord only (*secco*), but he sometimes used one or two other instruments (*stromentato*). He never used all the instruments at once, and for the most part they were reserved for special dramatic effects, or for instrumental interludes.

At first, opera was only possible in the houses of the wealthy nobility, but in 1637 the first public opera house was opened in Venice, and then the new art became immensely popular, and spread rapidly throughout Italy, with opera houses opening in every town. Audiences came to applaud their favourite singers; and words and drama were quite subordinate to singing and spectacle.

Alessandro Scarlatti (1660–1725) wrote a large number of popular operas towards the end of the century. He was the first to develop the distinctive features of *aria da capo* form (see p. 95). This appealed to the public, largely because it gave much opportunity for vocal display in the *da capo* section, when the singer was free to add any ornamentation he thought fit. By then, it had become the custom to write an overture at the beginning of the opera, and the style he adopted became known as the Italian overture (see. p. 87).

Opera spread rapidly from Italy into other European countries, though at first it was still sung in Italian. *Lully* (1632–1687), an Italian who had settled in France, was a famous court musician who led Louis XIV's violin band, and who collaborated in plays and ballets with the dramatist Molière. He wrote the first operas to French words, and he was more concerned with the quality of the libretto than were the Italian composers. He used *recitativo stromentato* rather than *secco*, and he carefully observed the natural rhythm of the French words. He liked to introduce a ballet into his operas, and, in addition, he wrote a number of separate ballets, in which he sometimes danced himself. You may know the aria 'Bois épais' from his opera 'Armide', because it appears in many school song books. Lully adopted the French kind of overture (see pp. 86, 87).

Lully influenced the English *Purcell* (c. 1659–1695), as French ideas were adopted at the English court. His one opera 'Dido and Aeneas' is still performed today. But it was not the first English opera. A masque of Ben Jonson's was set in the style of an opera as early as 1617. One of the most famous of the early English operas was 'The Siege of Rhodes', written in 1656 by five different composers, of whom one was William Lawes who wrote the music to Milton's masque 'Comus'; and in 1685 John Blow, Purcell's teacher, wrote 'Venus and Adonis', a chamber opera, which served as a model for 'Dido and Aeneas'. But opera was not as popular in England as in Italy and France.

The Growth of Instrumental Music in the Seventeenth Century

The growth of opera had a great influence on the rapid development of musical instruments. A solo voice is accompanied better by instruments than by other voices, as it stands out more. Also a variety of instruments gives plenty of tone contrast, and aids the dramatic effect of the music. So, during this century, the makers experimented, and began to provide more efficient instruments; the performers developed a better technique; and composers gradually learnt how to write in a distinctive instrumental style.

The violin family began to supersede the viol family, as its instruments were less clumsy and offered greater opportunities for virtuosity. Following on the great Italian makers of the seventeenth century, Amati, Guarneri, and Stradivari (see p. 3) came the first great violin performer, teacher and composer, *Corelli* (1653-1713). His life is summarised at the end of this chapter. See also the reference to his music on p. 10.

The harpsichord was used as a *continuo* to accompany the opera singers in *recitativo secco*, and was also thought of as the indispensable foundation of all orchestral combinations (see p. 8). But, in addition, composers began to write solos for keyboard instruments. The Elizabethan virginal composers have already been referred to. During the seventeenth century the Frenchman *Couperin* (1668-1733) wrote 27 suites of harpsichord pieces, called "ordres". The movements are mostly dance-like, and in binary form, though some are in rondo form with contrasting couplets. They have fanciful titles such as 'The Enchantress', 'Butterflies' and 'The little Windmills'. Couperin was an early writer of programme music. Purcell also wrote groups of harpsichord pieces which he called "lessons". See "Dances of the Suite" on p. 69, and the life of Purcell at the end of this chapter.

The Development of Tonality and Musical Form in the Seventeenth Century

In an opera a soloist was accompanied by supporting harmonies, not by equally important counterpoints. This resulted in a greater interest in chords and a development of the harmonic style of writing. The emotional effect of discords in Monteverdi's operas has been referred to on p. 109.

Again, in an operatic solo the accompanying parts had the same phrase lengths as the soloist, instead of interweaving parts with overlapping phrases, as in a madrigal. Modern ideas of phrase balance and cadences at regular intervals resulted from this.

The old modes were not so suited to harmony as are the major and minor scales, and they gradually died out during this century. The feeling for tonality that developed with the use of the major and minor scales led naturally to the art of modulation, which is an essential element in modern musical form.

Harmony in major and minor keys, with regular phrases and cadential endings, and modulation to related keys from a key centre, made possible the developments in musical form which are described in Chapter Seven. Binary form was mostly used for short movements, with rondo form or ritornello form for longer ones. The aria da capo form appeared occasionally in instrumental as well as in vocal music. The instrumental music of the seventeenth and early eighteenth century paved the way for the great developments which were to occur in the days of Haydn, and all can ultimately be traced back to the birth of opera as the root cause.

Biography and Chief Works of Arcangelo Corelli

1653. Born near Milan, of a patrician family.
1666. Went to Bologna for violin lessons.
1675–85. Travelled abroad, winning fame as a violinist. Attached to court of Elector of Bavaria for a time, and also visited Hanover.

1685. Settled in Rome. Published a book of 12 sonatas. Made a great reputation as violin teacher, performer and composer, and fame gradually spread throughout Europe. Moved in the highest circles of Roman society, and became permanent guest of Cardinal Ottoboni, living in his palace, and conducting his Monday concerts.

1708. Conducted a work for Handel when he visited Rome, but he was not used to the fiery style, and Handel snatched his violin from him, to show him how it should be played.

Visited Naples, where Alessandro Scarlatti was the leading musician, but did not play very well (started a piece in C major when it was in C minor), and was so humiliated that he left Naples immediately. On returning to Rome, he found that a new violinist had superseded him, and was so perturbed that his health began to fail.

1713. Died, leaving £6,000, and a fine collection of pictures.

Wrote 60 sonatas, most of them for two violins, 'cello and harpsichord continuo. Laid the foundations of future violin composition, though he never went beyond the third position.

Also wrote concerti grossi, which established this kind of orchestral writing. (See pp. 12, 75) Concise, lucid, dignified style, with good slow movements.

Wrote no other kinds of music.

Biography and Chief Works of Henry Purcell

c. 1659. Born in London, of a famous family of musicians. Father and uncle both Gentlemen of the Chapel Royal. Became a "Child" of the Chapel himself, under Captain Cooke.

1670. Composed music for the Chapel, when only 11.

1672. Cooke was succeeded by Pelham Humfrey, who had earlier been sent to France by Charles II to learn the new French style of music from Lully, and who encouraged it at the Chapel Royal.

Purcell stayed on after his voice had broken, acting as copyist, etc., and became a pupil of John Blow. Continued to compose songs and anthems.

1679. Succeeded Blow as organist of Westminster Abbey. (Blow may have made way for his brilliant pupil, and he took up the post again after Purcell's death.) Began to compose incidental music to plays. Also wrote odes for special occasions.

8

1681. Married, and eventually had six children, though three died in infancy.

1682. Appointed organist of Chapel Royal.

1683. First works published: 12 sonatas for two violins, 'cello and harpsichord. They are similar to those of Corelli, which were written about the same time, though they are less violinistic. Wrote his first ode for St Cecilia's day.

c. 1688–90. Wrote 'Dido and Aeneas', his only real opera, for the girls of Josiah Priest's boarding school at Chelsea. Continued to write music for plays, including Dryden's 'Diocletian' and 'King Arthur'. Also wrote music for an adaptation of Shakespeare's 'A Midsummer Night's Dream', called 'The Fairy Queen', in which no words of Shakespeare's were set!

1695. Died in Westminster, aged only 37. Buried beneath organ in Westminster Abbey. Tablet states that he "is gone to that Blessed Place where only his harmony can be exceeded."

Wrote much church music, including anthems such as 'Rejoice in the Lord alway', and 'O Praise God in His Holiness'. Often set the psalms. Rather theatrical and secular settings, based on French style. Fond of dotted rhythms, unexpected discords, and orchestral interludes. Regarded as discreet entertainment for the Court. Influenced Handel's choral music.

A large number of festival odes for special occasions, including three for St Cecilia's day, the greatest being 'Hail, bright Cecilia'.

Incidental music to many plays, such as 'Diocletian', 'King Arthur' (from which comes 'Fairest Isle'), 'The Libertine' (from which comes 'Nymphs and shepherds'). Also wrote many solo songs, in addition to those from his plays.

One real opera: 'Dido and Aeneas'. Contains several ground basses, including 'When I am laid in Earth', and a wonderful final chorus 'With drooping Wings, ye Cupids, Come'.

Instrumental music: fantasies for strings; sonatas for strings and harpsichord, including the 'Golden' sonata; some slight suites (lessons) for harpsichord, intended for educational purposes (including the popular 'Minuet in G').

Baroque

Chapter Fifteen

The Age of Bach and Handel

At the close of the seventeenth century two great musical giants, Bach and Handel, were born in 1685. They had, as their heritage, all the experiments and musical compositions of the seventeenth century; and just as Palestrina's work had been the climax to the great age of medieval polyphony, so the work of Bach and Handel was the consummation of the "new music", in the "Baroque" style, that had developed throughout the seventeenth century.

Opera

Italy still continued to be the chief home of opera, and opera in the Italian language, with Italian singers, was exported from there into other countries. It became very conventionalised, with the singers being considered more important than anyone else, including the composer, and being idolised as popular favourites, like the film stars of today.

But Frenchmen went on developing opera in their own language, with its own distinctive features, paying more attention to the words, the drama, and the dancing than did the Italians. *Rameau* (1683–1764) wrote a number of French operas towards the end of his life, of which the best-known is 'Castor and Pollux'. He also wrote many ballets, including 'Les Indes galantes'. In addition to his compositions, he is famous for a treatise on harmony, which analysed and explained the new ideas about chords and their inversions, tonality and key relationships.

But Rameau did not have it all his own way in France, though he was supported by his friend Voltaire. There were Frenchmen, including the great Rousseau, who disagreed with his theories and his operas, and who said that opera should be in the Italian style and the Italian language, as the French language was not suited to singing.   People took sides in this famous quarrel, which became known as the "Guerre des Bouffons".

Opera spread into Germany also, but at first it was Italian opera, sung in Italian.   Hamburg was the first place to produce opera in German.   *Handel* played the violin in the opera house there for a time, and even wrote one or two German operas.   But he preferred the Italian kind, and he travelled to Italy as a young man and produced operas there. Then, when he came to England, he did his best to popularise Italian opera in England.   He thought of himself mainly as an opera composer, and he wrote many Italian operas for production in London.   He imported Italian singers who sang in Italian, side by side with English singers who sang in English in the same opera!   There were a great many conventions about the number of singers, the type of arias they were to sing, and the part of the opera in which they were to sing them.   Male sopranos were common, and were the spoilt darlings of the public.   Although there are many lovely arias in Handel's operas which are still sung today, the operas are rarely performed in their entirety because they seem so artificial to us.   They brought Handel fame at the time, but they caused him to become bankrupt more than once, because of rival factions, a rival opera house, and a fickle public which did not really accept Italian opera. It was his lack of success in establishing Italian opera in England that made him turn to writing oratorio, the type of work for which he is, today, most famous.

Gluck (1714–1787) is the other great opera composer of this period.   He was a Bohemian who was educated in Prague, and travelled to Milan, London, Germany, Copenhagen and Paris before settling in Vienna when he was 35.   Where-ever he went he produced operas of the conventional Italian kind, and became famous for them.   But he began to have doubts about the artistic value of this kind of opera, and, encouraged by a new librettist, who had lived in Paris and heard French opera, he startled Vienna in 1762, when he was 48, by producing 'Orpheus' in a completely new style.

In 1767 he produced another similar opera, 'Alceste', and this time he wrote a preface explaining his theories. The true office of music was to serve poetry by means of expression and by following the situations of the story without interrupting the action. So the *da capo* aria was out of place, as was also the vocal *coloratura* which the Italians loved. He ceased to use the harpsichord and *recitativo secco*, and adopted a *stromentato* or *arioso* style which anticipated the continuous texture which was later adopted by Wagner.

In 1773 Gluck visited Paris, where his views were likely to be more sympathetically received. He produced French versions of 'Orpheus' and 'Alceste', as well as some new operas with French texts. But the French loved artistic controversy, and they set up an Italian composer in opposition to him, so that it seemed like a continuation of the *Guerre des Bouffons*. Partisans of one side hissed the operas of the other! But Gluck's reforms affected the whole course of the future history of opera, and laid the foundations for the work of Wagner. 'Orpheus' is still in the operatic repertoire.

Sacred Music *Oratorios*

Bach and *Handel* are the only composers of this period whose sacred music is much performed today. Bach lived all his life in Germany, and Handel settled in England, so that they both worked in Protestant countries. However, Bach wrote one great Latin mass in B minor, too long for liturgical purposes, but one of the greatest sacred works in existence. If it is compared with the masses of Palestrina, the effect of the developments in the seventeenth century will be realised. It is not modal, but uses major and minor keys, with modulation to related keys as an essential part of the formal structure; it has a polyphonic texture, as have Palestrina's masses, but unlike the sixteenth-century works, the interweaving melodies are based on a harmonic structure, with the primary triads as their foundation; and instead of being "a cappella" (i.e. unaccompanied), it uses quite a large orchestra. Strings are the foundation, but Bach sometimes uses a solo violin, oboe d'amore or horn to weave an additional melody round a solo voice, and he uses trumpets effectively in several choruses.   Every number in this great work has its beauties, but perhaps two of the most outstanding are the 'Crucifixus', with its heart-rending chorus built on a ground bass, and the 'Sanctus', which provides one of the most uplifting moments in the whole of choral music.

However, most of Bach's sacred choral music was in the form of cantatas, in which chorales played an essential part. The 'Christmas Oratorio' is really six cantatas strung together.   In addition he wrote four (?) settings of the Passion, including the great 'St Matthew'.   (See "Chorale", "Cantata", and "Passion Music" on pp. 97–99 for further information about his works for these media.)

Handel's sacred music that has survived is mainly in the form of oratorios, though he wrote quite a number of anthems, including those dedicated to his English patron, the Duke of Chandos.   Most of his oratorios were indistinguishable in style from his operas, making much use of the *da capo* aria, and having a theatrical style.   He could use a larger chorus, however, than was possible in his operas, and he made effective use of this, sometimes for reflective and sometimes for dramatic purposes.   'Israel in Egypt' uses the chorus to a great extent, and it, together with 'Judas Maccabeus' and 'Samson' are still frequently performed today.   But 'Messiah' stands apart, as being much more deeply felt.   It has few *da capo* arias, and creates an effective balance between aria, recitative and chorus.

Like Bach, Handel uses modern tonality, a polyphonic texture based on a harmonic structure, and an accompanying orchestra.   But his style is simpler, and therefore easier to sing and to listen to.   He has a strong sense of the dramatic and he is more concerned with the broad effect of the whole than with giving the loving care which Bach lavished on every detail.

Instrumental Music

Both *Bach* and *Handel* wrote concerti grossi similar to those of Corelli (see p. 12 for further details).   They also wrote a number of other orchestral works, such as overtures, suites and concertos for solo instruments, and chamber music for various solo instruments or combinations of them. The continuo was present in all of these works, except for a few suites which Bach wrote for violin alone and 'cello alone (see pp. 69–76 for details of form and style). If we compare these works with the instrumental fantasies of the Elizabethans we can see how much they are indebted to the innovations of the seventeenth century. The violin family has completely ousted the viol family, and a large combination of instruments, called an orchestra, has come into being. Movements are much longer and more highly organised, largely because of the development of tonality and the possibilities of key contrasts. Instrumental music of this period is quite often heard at concerts today, while Elizabethan instrumental music is a rarity.

In addition to the use of the harpsichord for continuo purposes in all chamber, orchestral and accompanied choral music, there was a growing literature for it as a solo instrument. Much of this music could be played on the clavichord as well, though the harpsichord would always be used in a large room (see pp. 6–8 for a description of these instruments).

Handel wrote quite a large body of harpsichord music, including suites, sonatas and fugues, but it is rather thin and bare. He added embellishments and improvisations when performing these works in public himself. On the whole he did not pay a great deal of attention to his harpsichord music, and it does not form part of his best work.

But the situation is quite different with Bach. He loved the keyboard instruments, particularly the intimate little clavichords, and he surrounded himself with them in his home. Page 8 explains how his 48 preludes and fugues, were composed to demonstrate the advantages of equal temperament, and there are many references to them on pp. 64–68: while pp. 70–71 refer to his keyboard suites. Bach's clavier music is a most important side of his work. It is usually played on the piano today, and is an indispensable part of every pianist's repertoire.

One other clavier composer of the period must be mentioned: *Domenico Scarlatti*, the son of the opera composer. He was born in the same year as Bach and Handel, and died in 1757. He was a Neapolitan, but he travelled a good deal in Italy, and in Spain where he finally settled. He was the first composer to make a study of the particular character-istics of the harpsichord, and his pieces have a brilliance and a delicacy that delight audiences today. He was fond of effects gained by crossing the hands, though eventually he got too fat to play them with ease! He wrote at least 555 sonatas, but they were all short and in one movement, usually in binary form. His other works, mainly operas and church music, are now rarely heard.

The last instrument to be discussed here is the organ. Handel left a number of organ concertos, but the organ part is sketchy, as he added his own improvisations when giving performances of the works. They were secular "show" pieces, often played between sections of an oratorio, as a relaxation. Bach's organ pieces, on the contrary, are a most important side of his work. He wrote a large number of preludes and fugues, toccatas, sonatas, fantasies and choral preludes, some quite easy, others very difficult. Bach is considered to be the greatest of all organ composers.

Biography and Chief Works of Johann Sebastian Bach

1685. Born at Eisenach in Thuringia, youngest child of a pro-fessional musician, one of an outstandingly musical family, 38 of whom are mentioned in Grove's dictionary. Both parents died when he was 9. Eldest brother (also a musician) then housed him and taught him the Clavier. Spent six months copying a forbidden MS. by candlelight. Copy confiscated when discovered.

1700. Left his brother to become paid chorister at Lüneberg, 200 miles away. While there made several visits on foot to Hamburg, 30 miles away, to hear famous organist. Also went to hear French chamber music. Began to compose.

1703. After a short period as a violinist in Weimar's court orchestra, was appointed organist at Arnstadt. Got leave of absence to visit Lübeck, to hear the famous organist Buxtehude, and probably had lessons from him. Great stimulus to organ composition. Reprimanded on his return for staying too long, for playing elaborate music in the Arnstadt services and for allowing a female cousin (whom he married a year later) to sing in the church.

1707. Post as organist at Mühlhausen. Religious dissensions made post difficult.

1708–1717. First important post, at *Weimar*—the Weimar period. Court organist to Duke, and later concert-master. Wrote much fine organ music, and became famous as organist. Also composed cantatas.

1717–1723. The *Cöthen* period. Conductor of court orchestra. Therefore wrote mainly instrumental chamber and orchestral works: Brandenburg concertos; orchestral suites; English and French Clavier suites; first half of "48" intended for his children's education, etc. First wife died in 1720, while Bach was away from home. The following year married Anna Magdalena and eventually had 20 children. Attempted to meet Handel, but never managed it.

1723–1750. The *Leipzig* period. Cantor and teacher at St Thomas's choir school, which supplied the music for the town's four churches. Two churches had elaborate choral music with orchestral accompaniment, cantatas being performed at each on alternate Sundays. Involved in controversies with the University, the Town Council and the Headmasters of the choir school (called Rectors). Wrote many cantatas, the B minor mass, the St Matthew Passion, the second book of the '48'. Happy home life, surrounded by musical children, several of whom became famous.

1747. Visited court of Frederick the Great, where his son, Carl Philipp Emanuel, was in the King's service. Tried the king's new pianos, and amazed him by his powers of improvisation.

1749. Began to lose eyesight, as a result of copying so much music throughout his life. After operation lost it completely.

1750. Died.

A devout Christian, who thought of music as primarily for the service of God. Gave great care to every detail. A great contrapuntist, whose works reveal new beauties every time they are heard afresh. Melodies less "vocal" than Handel's. Wrote all types of music except opera, which was too superficial to interest him. Already considered old-fashioned by the time he died, as a new, less contrapuntal style was coming into being.

But Bach's music does not age. Its strength, vigour and fresh-ness has continued to appeal to musicians and music lovers of all ages.

Many sacred choral works, including 5 sets of cantatas for every Sunday and holy day in the year. Over 200 extant. 4 (?) Passions ('St Matthew' the greatest). 'Christmas Oratorio', 'Mass in B minor', 6 motets in German.

27 secular cantatas, including 'Peasant Cantata', 'Coffee and Cupid'.

Organ music: fantasias; toccatas, including 'Toccata and Fugue in D minor'; preludes and fugues, including 'St Anne Fugue'; choral preludes.

Clavier music: 'The well-tempered Clavier' (the '48'); 6 partitas; 6 French suites; 6 English suites; 2- and 3-part Inventions. Other miscellaneous works, such as 'Italian Concerto'.

'The Art of Fugue' was written in open score, but was probably intended to be played on a keyboard instrument.

Orchestral music: 'Brandenburg' concertos (see p. 12 for details); concertos for violin, etc., including double violin concerto, concertos for 1–4 harpsichords; orchestral suites.

Chamber music: solo suites for violin and 'cello: trios, etc.

Biography and Chief Works of George Frideric Handel

1685. Born in Halle, Saxony. Father an elderly barber-surgeon, determined that his son should do well in life, and therefore against so precarious a living as that of a musician. But allowed him to have music lessons.

1702. Entered Halle University, to study law.

1703. Left University, and went to Hamburg, where he played violin and then harpsichord at the opera house. Continued his musical training.

1705. Wrote two operas for the Hamburg opera house.

1706–10. Travelled to Italy, visiting Florence, Rome, Venice and Naples. Wrote a number of works and had Italian operas produced in Florence and Venice. Met Corelli and D. and A. Scarlatti.

1710. Appointed Kapellmeister to the Elector of Hanover, who agreed he should be allowed to visit England. Arrived in London, and at once produced a successful opera. Returned to Hanover.

1712. Another visit to England, again successful. Queen Anne settled a pension on him. Stayed on, overstaying his leave.

1714. Queen Anne died. Elector of Hanover became George I of England. He forgave Handel's truancy almost immediately, confirmed and doubled his pension and attended the performance of his opera 'Rinaldo'.

1715—1717. Wrote music for two or more royal water parties on the Thames. Music collected and published in 1740, as 'Water Music'.

1718. Made chapel master to the Duke of Chandos, for whom he wrote the Chandos Anthems.

1719. Became a director of a new opera venture "The Royal Academy of Music" which gave performances at the King's Theatre. Went abroad in search of Italian singers.

1720–1728. Opera house produced Handel's operas (and others) every season, but gradually ran into difficulties, caused by quarrels between singers, the opening of a rival opera house patronised by the Prince of Wales in opposition to the King, and finally the success of an English ballad opera 'The Beggar's Opera'. Ended in bankruptcy.

1729. Started again, under the patronage of the new king, George II, but the new Prince of Wales started in rivalry. Struggled on till 1737, when he was forced to close the theatre. But the first oratorio, 'Esther', and the English pastoral 'Acis and Galatea', performed at this theatre, in costume, without action, were quite successful.

1738. Obtained £1,000 by means of a benefit concert to pay off his creditors.

1739. Turned to oratorio, as being more satisfactory financially, and produced 'Saul' and 'Israel in Egypt'. Used English singers, who were easier to control than Italians. Oratorios were performed in the theatre, many in Covent Garden.

1741. Wrote 'Messiah' in 23 days.

1742. 'Messiah' produced in Dublin with other works, all very successful.

1743. 'Samson' given eight successful performances in London, but 'Messiah' a failure. 'Dettingen Te Deum' performed in Chapel Royal.

1746. Wrote 'Judas Maccabeus'.

1750. 'Messiah' successfully performed for Foundling Hospital. Thereafter gave successful yearly performances of 'Messiah' for this charity.

1752. Began to go blind, and, after three operations, lost his sight in 1753. But still continued active.

1759. Presided at organ in performance of 'Messiah' at Covent Garden. Died eight days later. Buried in Westminster Abbey.

Strong-minded; determined to succeed; made the most of every opportunity that came his way; always busy and in the thick of struggles; kind hearted, generous and honourable. Never married.

Often used material from his early works in later ones, and, in addition, sometimes made unacknowledged borrowings from other composers. Greatest qualities are his feeling for vocal line, which makes his arias ideal teaching material for singers, and his broad dramatic choral writing.

Wrote many operas, such as 'Rinaldo', 'Julius Caesar', 'Scipio'. Have not lived, but many arias from them still sung today.

Secular choral works, such as 'Acis and Galatea', 'Alexander's Feast', 'Ode for St Cecilia's Day'.

19 oratorios. The first English one was 'Esther'; the greatest are 'Saul', 'Israel in Egypt', 'Messiah', 'Samson' and 'Judas Maccabeus'.

Good deal of church music, including 'Chandos' anthems, 4 coronation anthems for accession of George II, and 'Dettingen Te Deum'.

A large number of cantatas and other vocal music.

Orchestral music, including 'Water Music', 'Fireworks Music', concerti grossi, organ concertos.

Instrumental music for various combinations.

Harpsichord music, suites, fugues, etc.

Chapter Sixteen

The Viennese Period

Bach died in 1750 and Handel in 1759. Haydn and Mozart, the next pair of great composers, were born in 1732 and 1756 respectively, and the chief musical centre switches to Vienna, where they both lived and worked. Beethoven and Schubert were to follow on in the same town, and this great period of musical activity is often called "The Viennese Period". During its course, sonata form and the other kindred forms were evolved, the string quartet was born, the modern orchestra was founded, and the symphony and concerto, as we know them today, were established.

Development of Form

Bach's contrapuntal style was already considered old-fashioned before he died, and his son *Carl Philipp Emanuel*, who was at the court of Frederick the Great, and later had a post in Hamburg, seemed, to his generation, to be more important than his father. He experimented with a new style of writing, consisting of a single, ornate melody with a simple harmonic accompaniment. He was interested in the formal aspect, and his Clavier sonatas influenced Haydn considerably. They were usually in three movements, quick, slow, quick. The opening movement contained a first section with a string of short themes or figures in the tonic key, followed by others in either the dominant or relative major key; while the second section, though it began in this related key, went some distance afield, with both keys and themes, before it returned to the original string of themes, now all in the tonic key. In this plan we see the first hints of a contrasted second subject or group of subjects in a related key, and a development section, two ideas which Haydn, Mozart and Beethoven were later to put to good use.

C. P. E. Bach is usually considered the forerunner of sonata form. (For further details see "The Evolution of Sonata Form" on pp. 80–88.)

Haydn experimented a good deal with musical form, and although one thinks of sonata form as being established by him, it is important to realise that many of his movements are a very free mixture of several forms, which cannot be given a particular "label". *Mozart*, on the whole, was less adventurous in this matter. By the time of Beethoven the outlines of the different forms that were used in sonatas and symphonies and similar works had become accepted in the musical world, and Haydn's and Mozart's works, together with those of contemporaries of lesser importance, laid this foundation. (For further details of the different forms, see Chapter Nine.)

Beethoven, then, had established forms ready at hand. He enlarged them, but did not greatly change them. His development sections, his codas, his modulatory experiments, his scherzos, and his variations in the number and order of the movements are all noteworthy. (Again, see Chapter Nine for further details.)

Schubert, too, accepted the standard forms, and was content to be rather conventional in this matter. He tended to be too prolix, but his modulations were adventurous, colourful and well managed.

The Piano and the Piano Sonata

During this period the harpsichord was gradually dying out, and the piano was gaining the ascendancy. The sustaining pedal was invented, the range was extended, the instrument developed greater sonority, and it became very popular.

All the four chief Viennese composers, Haydn, Mozart, Beethoven and Schubert, wrote sonatas for the piano. Mozart's and Beethoven's form an essential part of the pianist's repertory, and many people gain their first impression of the difference between Mozart's and Beethoven's styles through a study of their sonatas.

Haydn developed the sonata from what he found in the works of C. P. E. Bach, though in his case it is the development of sonata form, rather than his actual keyboard compositions, that are important, and most of them were probably still played on the harpsichord. He simplified the contrapuntal style of his predecessors, and wrote melodic, clearly-defined subjects. His sonatas usually have two or three movements; and when there are three the middle movement is more often an adagio than a minuet, though the last movement is then usually a dance form such as a minuet with variations or a rondo.

Mozart's 24 sonatas are of rather unequal merit, and many of them are early works. They are almost invariably in three movements, the usual plan being an allegro in sonata form, a slow movement, and a rondo. In addition, he wrote a number of isolated sonata movements, and other piano works such as variations, rondos and fantasies. But his piano writing is seen at its best in his piano concertos. In Mozart's time the piano had a light and delicate touch; but Beethoven required greater sonority, and encouraged this development with piano manufacturers.

Beethoven's 32 sonatas are a most important side of his work. They are longer, more dramatic and more passionate than Mozart's, and bear evidence of his development through the "three periods" of his life. He writes magnificent development sections and long codas, and his transitions are an integral part of the movement, instead of the rather obvious punctuation points that often occur in Mozart's sonatas. The four-movement plan is common, the additional movement frequently being a scherzo. But Beethoven experiments with the number and order of his movements. Everyone knows his so-called 'Moonlight' sonata, which begins with a slow movement. Other famous sonatas are the 'Pathétique', the 'Waldstein' and the 'Appassionata'. He also wrote several fine sets of variations for the piano.

Schubert's 22 sonatas have occasional weaknesses, such as an unpianistic lay-out, but they contain some lovely movements, with beautiful and unexpected but delightful

modulations.   His impromptus and Moments Musicaux
are popular examples of his other works for piano.

The Growth of the String Quartet

Haydn was the first great composer to write quartets for
two violins, viola and 'cello, though other composers began
to use this medium about the same time.   Compare this
combination with that of the string sonata of Corelli's day,
with its two melodic violin parts, its bass played by the 'cello,
and its harmonic filling in, provided by the harpsichord
continuo part.

Haydn was invited for a long visit to a country house at
Weinzierl when he was 23, and he happened to find four
string players there, so wrote his first string quartets for them,
applying what he had learnt from the study of C. P. E. Bach's
sonatas to this medium.

C. P. E. Bach's sonatas had consisted of three movements,
quick, slow, quick, none of them being dance movements.
But Haydn liked the minuet so much that, from the beginning, he began to add it to his chamber and orchestral works.
Many of his first quartets were in five movements, with two
minuets, but eventually he established a four movement
scheme with a minuet for the third movement.

His earliest quartets, like the string sonatas of Corelli,
tended to treat the violins as being the important melodic
instruments.   But the lack of a harmonic continuo background made the viola and 'cello lines more prominent, and
gradually Haydn realised that they, too, could have interesting melodic parts.   You may have heard or played the
popular "serenade" from his quartet in F, op. 3, no. 5,
which has the tune entirely in the first violin while the others
play a pizzicato accompaniment.   Compare it with the even
better-known air and variations from the 'Emperor'
quartet, op, 76, no. 3, in which each instrument has the tune
in turn.

All the great Viennese composers, *Haydn*, *Mozart*, *Beethoven*
and *Schubert* wrote string quartets, and together they established the medium and founded a literature for it which has

made it the greatest and most important of all chamber music combinations. But they all wrote for other chamber music combinations as well. (See "Chamber Music" on pp. 85–86.)

The Development of the Orchestra

Stamitz (1717–1757) directed a famous orchestra at Mannheim and wrote a number of symphonies for it. But although the orchestral and symphonic traditions he established affected the work of Haydn, and even more of Mozart, his music was not the work of a genius, and Haydn's symphonies are the earliest that are still regularly heard today.

The same Weinzierl visit which gave *Haydn* the opportunity to write his first string quartet also made it possible for him to experiment with larger groups when they happened to be available: for example, there were two horn players among his host's huntsmen. He wrote a number of slight works, in several movements, which he indiscriminately called divertimenti, cassations or symphonies, often for oboes, horns and strings. At first the style was very simple, and not clearly differentiated from chamber music.

The greatest step forward, however, took place when Haydn was appointed Kapellmeister to Prince Esterhazy at Eisenstadt. Here he was gradually able to increase the size of the orchestra and to have daily rehearsals. The Prince soon built a large palace, "Esterhaz", which rivalled Versailles, and had two theatres attached. It was in the heart of the country, so there were no distractions, and Haydn devoted all his attention to composing and conducting music for his patron, and discovering the best way of writing for an orchestra. He began to be conscious of the tone qualities of the different instruments, and of the possibilities of using them for providing contrast. Hearing the young Mozart's symphonies, with their greater delicacy and variety of tone colour, also affected Haydn's later symphonies. (See "The Symphonies of Haydn and Mozart" on pp. 24 and 26.)

9

Mozart's first attempts at orchestral writing owed much to Haydn's, and both used the clarinet later, when it became possible to get players. *Beethoven* and *Schubert* began to use trombones occasionally, even in their symphonies. But fundamentally the essential features of orchestral writing were laid down by Haydn, and formed the basis for all nineteenth century orchestral composition.

The Development of the Symphony

Haydn's experiments in musical form, and in the composition of the orchestra, resulted in the symphony as we know it today. He wrote 104 symphonies, though the earliest ones were very slight. The later ones include a set of six "Paris" and twelve "London" symphonies. Some of his symphonies have been given titles, such as the 'Farewell'; the 'Hen' and the 'Paris' of the Paris set; the 'Oxford'; and the 'Surprise', the 'Military', the 'Clock', the 'Drumroll', and the 'London' from the London set. His best symphonies were written at the end of his life, after the death of Mozart, and show the influence of the younger composer.

Mozart, twenty-four years younger than Haydn, and a devoted admirer of his, began by writing symphonies similar to Haydn's; but soon he was showing individual touches, particularly as regards orchestration, and the delicacy and sensitivity shown in the last three of his 41 symphonies, the 'Jupiter', the 'E♭ major' and the 'G minor', make them great masterpieces of orchestral writing.

Beethoven found the symphonic pattern well established, and, as with his piano sonatas, he enlarged it and made it more dramatic, so that his 9 great symphonies are all popular in the concert hall today. The first two belong to his "first period", when he was much affected by Haydn and Mozart, but even they have passages that could have been written by no earlier composer. The third, the 'Eroica', written in honour of Napoleon, is a gigantic work, about an hour in length, while the fifth, in C minor, and the sixth, the 'Pastoral', are two of the most popular in the concert repertory. The ninth symphony belongs to his "third period". It, too, is very long, and introduces the innovation of a chorus in the last movement.

Schubert wrote 11 symphonies, of which one is lost and another is unfinished. But the 'Unfinished', though only possessing two movements, is the most popular of all. At the end of his short life he wrote the 'Great' C major, a very long but beautiful symphony, over which he took much greater pains than usual, and this is perhaps his greatest work.

The Development of the Concerto

During this period the concerto adopted the new forms used in the sonata and the symphony, and the new style of orchestral writing, though it also developed some characteristics of its own, largely through the influence of Mozart. It became much more of a vehicle for the display of virtuosity on the part of the solo performer than the earlier concertos had been, and works for more than one solo instrument became more rare. (For details of this form see pp. 88–90.)

Haydn wrote a number of concertos for the Clavier, the violin and the 'cello, but, apart from the 'cello concerto in D major, they are rarely performed. There is also a very popular trumpet concerto. He contributed much less to the development of the concerto than to the quartet and the symphony.

Mozart wrote many concertos, for many different instruments. His violin concertos were mostly written before he was 21, though they are still frequently played. He wrote 25 piano concertos, at different periods of his life, many of which are very fine works and still regularly played today. He was the first great writer of piano concertos, and laid the foundation for the style. He also wrote a number of concertos for wind instruments, including two for flute, one each for oboe, clarinet and bassoon, four for horn and one for flute and harp. Although they are not often heard at concerts they are mostly obtainable on records, and provide one of the best means of becoming familiar with the sound of each instrument and of its capabilities in solo work.

Beethoven wrote fewer concertos, but all are important works. There are five for piano, including the 'Emperor': one for violin; and a triple concerto for piano, violin and 'cello, which is rarely performed. He gave the orchestra a more interesting part than Mozart had done; in the piano concertos in G and E♭ (the 'Emperor'), he connected the second and third movements; and in his last concerto, the Emperor, he wrote out a cadenza, instead of leaving the soloist to make up his own. From then onwards, composers almost invariably wrote their own cadenzas, though some of the more recent concertos, such as the piano concertos of Brahms, do not contain a cadenza at all.

Schubert wrote no concertos, but passing reference should be made to *Paganini* and *Spohr*, who wrote virtuoso concertos for the violin which are still used by students as practice works.

Opera

Haydn wrote quite a number of operas for Prince Esterhazy's opera-house, including some for his puppet theatre, but they are slight works, and are rarely performed today.

Mozart's operas, however, are a most important side of his work, and, together with those of Verdi and Wagner, provide the main repertory of the modern opera house. He inherited the reforms of Gluck, whose operas he heard in Vienna, and the dramatic effect of his operas was enhanced by his fine sense of characterisation, and by his magnificently built up finales to each act.

He began to write operas when he was only 11 years old, and 'Bastien and Bastienne', written when he was 12, is still performed today. His greatest operas are the Italian grand opera 'Idomeneo', containing choruses and ballets; the German *singspiel* (a light opera with spoken dialogue) 'The Abduction from the Seraglio'; the Italian light operas 'The Marriage of Figaro', 'Don Giovanni' and 'Cosi fan Tutte'; and the German singspiel 'The Magic Flute', which was written at the end of his life for a little theatre in the suburbs of Vienna. This last opera has a nonsensical and confused story, but is full of lovely music and is a landmark in the history of opera written in the German language.

Beethoven wrote only one opera, 'Fidelio', and this, too, was in German. He always hoped to write some more, but could never find a suitable libretto, for he would only consider great and noble subjects. The heroine of 'Fidelio' is a noble and faithful wife "Leonora", who sets out to save her wrongfully imprisoned husband, and the opera has many fine moments, though it is not very often performed today. Beethoven was so self-critical that he wrote four different overtures to this opera in the attempt to find the ideal form. They are now known as 'Leonora' nos. 1, 2 and 3, and 'Fidelio', which last finally became the one to be attached to the opera.

Schubert wrote a number of operas, but in every case the libretti were so poor that they failed to inspire him, and they are rarely performed today. He also wrote incidental music to three plays, and the overture and entr'actes to 'Rosamunde' are still popular.

Sacred Music

Haydn, Mozart, Beethoven and *Schubert* were all Catholics who wrote masses for their patrons, but, for the most part, they seem rather secular, and are not much used in church worship. Haydn's were cheerful works, for he said that at the thought of God his heart leaped for joy, and he could not help his music doing the same. Most of Mozart's church music, including his masses, was composed for the Archbishop of Salzburg, and is rather conventional in style. But the Requiem Mass, which he left unfinished on his death bed, is much more deeply felt. Beethoven's greatest sacred work is his 'Solemn Mass' in D major, written on a large scale for public performance in the concert room. Schubert's 6 masses, like his other church music, are rather perfunctory and are rarely performed, though the one in G is quite popular.

The best-known sacred work of the Viennese period is Haydn's oratorio 'The Creation'. It was the fruit of his second visit to London, where he heard and was impressed by Handel's oratorios. He was given an English libretto, compiled from the Bible and Milton's "Paradise Lost", and took it back to Vienna, where he had it translated into German. He was 64 when he started to compose the work and he said "Never was I so pious. I knelt down each day and prayed God to give me strength to finish the work." It contains some delightfully vivid tone pictures, and the orchestra plays a much more important part than in any oratorio of Handel's.

The Art Song

Haydn and *Mozart* both wrote a large number of songs, but most of them were simple, rather formal melodies, with an unimportant accompaniment, and the poems which they set were usually rather uninteresting. By *Beethoven's* time the piano had become a much more expressive instrument, able to add appreciably to the effect of a song, and Germany was producing fine lyric poetry, so that the stage was set for the modern art song. But Beethoven was an instrumental rather than a vocal writer, so that, although he wrote many songs, he did not realise the new potentialities. It was *Schubert* who, with his gift of melody and his spontaneous reaction to poetry, brought the art song to birth. His settings of Goethe's 'Gretchen at the Spinning Wheel' and 'The Erl King', written when only in his 'teens, are amazing artistic creations. The form grows out of the words, and the accompaniment adds enormously to the artistic effect. He wrote 600 songs in his short life, some in stanzas, more in a continuous whole (*durchcomponirt*); some using poems of great poets such as Goethe, Schiller and Heine, more using rather second-rate poems written by his personal friends. But all of them got to the essence of the poetry and expressed it through the voice and the piano in a wonderful new way. As far as song writing is concerned, Schubert belongs to the new Romantic era, and he paved the way for the great German *Lieder* writers later in the century.

Biography and Chief Works of Franz Joseph Haydn

1732. Born at Rohrau, in Lower Austria. Father a wheel-wright; mother a cook. He was one of 12 children.

1740. Entered the Vienna choir school, because of his good voice. His younger brother Michael also entered later, and took Joseph's place when his voice broke.

1745. Left choir school and attempted to live in Vienna by teaching music and accompanying for a singing teacher. But they were lean years. Had had little instruction in composition, but discovered C. P. E. Bach's clavier sonatas and learnt much from studying them. Gradually acquired more text books and taught himself.

1755. Invited to stay at country house at Weinzierl to perform and compose music for the players he found there. Wrote his first string quartets and other chamber music, and his first works for a small orchestra: divertimenti, cassations and miniature symphonies.

1756. Returned to Vienna and gradually became known as a performer and teacher.

1759. Obtained a small post as music director to a count, at a salary of £20 a year, where he had more opportunities of composing for a small orchestra. Married the following year, but marriage unhappy and childless.

1761. Appointed second Kapellmeister to Esterhazy, a wealthy and musical Hungarian prince, who had an orchestra of his own at Eisenstadt, his country seat. Later became first Kapellmeister. The orchestra was enlarged and rehearsed every day. He wrote 30 symphonies and many slighter orchestral and chamber works in this period.

1766. The prince built an enormous new summer residence "Esterhaz", as grand as Versailles, in the middle of remote, marshy country. Had two theatres in the grounds, for which Haydn wrote operas, and music for puppet plays. Wrote another 30 symphonies and much other orchestral and chamber music. Prince stayed at Esterhaz for a large part of the year, but Haydn welcomed the seclusion, as it gave him the opportunity to compose and experiment, and he was forced to become original. Fame spread throughout Europe, and many of his works published.

1781. Met Mozart in Vienna. They continued to meet occasionally when Haydn visited Vienna. Each admired the other, and learnt from the other's compositions, Mozart's musical forms becoming more free, and Haydn's orchestration becoming more full of colour.

1790. Esterhazy died, leaving Haydn a pension. New prince dismissed orchestra. Haydn settled in Vienna. Had previously been asked to visit London but had not felt he could leave Prince. Being now free, he came to London on the invitation of a violinist, Salomon. Received with acclamation. Given a Doctorate at Oxford. Paid many visits. Produced first 6 of London symphonies. Many other works performed. Stayed two years.

1792. Travelled through Bonn on way home and met Beethoven, who followed him to Vienna for lessons.

1794. Another visit to London. The second 6 London symphonies commissioned. Made sufficient money to keep him in his old age. Heard and was impressed by Handel's oratorios. Took libretto of 'Creation' back with him.

1795. Returned to Vienna, living there for the rest of his life, but visiting Esterhaz each summer.

1797. Composed 'Emperor's Hymn', the Austrian national anthem, and incorporated it in the 'Emperor' quartet. Composed 'The Creation', which was performed everywhere. Old age passed in Vienna, among friends, revered by everyone; world famous.

1809. Died in Vienna when invading forces of Napoleon were in occupation.

A simple, genial person, whom everyone loved. Affectionately known as Papa Haydn. Strong sense of humour. Devout catholic. His development of sonata form, the quartet, and the modern symphony make him a figure of great historical importance. Excellent sense of form made it possible for him to produce unexpected irregularities of phrase length and unusual formal shapes which yet create a satisfying balance. Love of folk-like tunes, particularly in finales.

Much chamber music, including 83 string quartets, some with nicknames such as the 'Bird', the 'Lark', the 'Razor', the 'Emperor'.

Much orchestral music, including 104 symphonies, the best-known being the 'Farewell', the 6 'Paris' symphonies, the

'Oxford' and the 12 'London' symphonies, including the 'Surprise', the 'Military', the 'Clock', the 'Drum Roll' and the 'London'. Many smaller orchestral works, divertimenti, cassations, etc. Concertos not often played today, except for one 'cello concerto and the trumpet concerto.

Oratorios: 'The Creation' and 'The Seasons'. Much church music, including 14 masses.

A number of slight and rather unimportant operas, and puppet operas.

60 Clavier sonatas, 8 of them lost. Other small Clavier works, not of great importance.

Large number of songs, including arrangements of folk songs, many of them Scottish; canons and rounds. Rarely heard today.

Biography and Chief Works of Wolfgang Amadeus Mozart

1756. Born in Salzburg. Father, Leopold, was violinist and court musician to Archbishop of Salzburg, and wrote a famous treatise on violin playing. Sister Marianne and Wolfgang were both child prodigies.

1762. Already composing and playing violin and Clavier. Taught by father, who took children to play at courts of Munich and Vienna.

1763. Started a 3-year tour of Europe. Visited courts of Versailles and London. Met J. C. Bach in London, gave many concerts there, and composed his first symphony. Then on to the court at The Hague, and other places in Holland, France and Switzerland before returning home.

1768. Visited Vienna and had opera 'Bastien and Bastienne' performed.

1769. Two-year Italian tour. Heard Allegri's 'Miserere' in Sistine chapel, Rome, twice, then wrote it out from memory. Continued to make long concert tours with his father until he was 21, frequently visiting Italy and Vienna, being fêted wherever he went and producing many compositions. Occasional periods at home in Salzburg, which became increasingly irksome, as the new Archbishop, in whose service he was, was unpopular and unappreciative of his gifts.

1777. Left service of Archbishop. Travelled with mother to Mannheim, where heard famous orchestra and a new instrument, the clarinet. Fell in love with Aloysia Weber, a singer, cousin of the composer, Weber. Father ordered him to Paris.

1778. Arrived in Paris, but little interest taken in him—now too old to excite comment as a prodigy.   Wrote 'Paris' symphony. Mother died there.

1779. Returned to service of Archbishop.   But found it so uncongenial that left two years later, and settled permanently in Vienna.   Met Haydn.   Each greatly admired the other.

1782. Married Constanze Weber, sister of Aloysia, who had married someone else.   She proved to be a bad manager, and they lived in great poverty.   Always hoping for a regular, lucrative appointment, but never got one.   Gave lessons and concerts and continued to compose operas, symphonies, concertos, etc.

1786. 'Marriage of Figaro' produced in Vienna, to enthusiastic audiences.   Then produced in Prague, where he went to hear it performed.   Wrote the 'Prague' symphony and 'Don Giovanni' for this town, and was very happy in the appreciative atmosphere.

1787. Continued living in poverty in Vienna, but wrote his 3 greatest symphonies, the E♭, the G minor and the 'Jupiter' in six weeks in 1788.   Added wind parts to Handel's works, including 'Messiah', for performances in Vienna.

1789. Visited Dresden, Leipzig (where he played on Bach's organ), and Berlin, in hopes of making more money.   But little financial result.   Both he and his wife constantly ailing.

1791. Spurred   himself   to   final   effort.   'Magic   Flute'. 'Requiem', commissioned by mysterious stranger, left unfinished on his death bed.   Buried in pauper's grave.

A wonderful prodigy, who, after a most successful childhood, was neglected on reaching maturity, and who was prematurely worn out by travelling and poverty.   Enjoyed billiards and dancing.   An ardent freemason.   A fine pianist, particularly good at extemporising.   Also an organist and violinist, though preferred to play the viola in chamber music.   Disliked teaching. A prolific composer, who was able to conceive a complete composition in his head before writing it down.   Continued with chamber music on Haydn's lines; further developed the symphony, adding a finer orchestral colouring; originated the modern concerto; wrote a number of fine operas.   Work characterised by graceful sensitivity and great clarity of style.   Fond of chromatic melodic decorations, and occasional chromatic harmonies.

600 compositions preserved, of which few were printed in his lifetime. Of varied merit. Many "occasional" compositions, written without enthusiasm. Köchel collected them, hence "K" numbers.

39 symphonies, the last and greatest being the E♭, K 543; the G minor, K 550; and the 'Jupiter', K 551. Many other orchestral compositions, divertimenti, serenades, etc. ('Eine kleine Nacht Musik' is a serenade.)

25 piano concertos, and a number for other instruments, including 5 for violin, 2 for flute, 1 each for oboe, clarinet and bassoon, 4 for horn, and 1 for flute and harp.

A large amount of chamber music, including 23 string quartets, 2 flute quartets, 1 oboe quartet, 2 piano quartets, and a clarinet quintet.

24 piano sonatas and other piano works, such as variations, rondos and fantasies. Many are comparatively early works, and overfull of mannerisms.

Large number of operas, the best-known being 'Idomeneo', 'The Abduction from the Seraglio', 'The Marriage of Figaro', 'Don Giovanni', 'Cosi fan Tutte' and 'The Magic Flute'.

A quantity of church music, masses, etc., the finest works being the Requiem Mass, the C minor Mass, 'Exultate Jubilate', and 'Ave Verum'.

Biography and Chief Works of Ludwig van Beethoven

1770. Born in Bonn. Father a chorister in Elector of Cologne's chapel, a thriftless drunkard. Two younger brothers. Had little education or social culture, but, on showing signs of musical ability, his father tried to force and exploit his gifts.

1782. Became deputy court organist and theatre accompanist.

1787. Visited Vienna where he improvised before Mozart and may have had a few lessons from him. But hurried home, as his mother was dying. Stayed in Bonn for the next five years, where he had to run the home, as his father's drunkenness had caused his dismissal. Continued in service of Elector, playing in court and opera orchestra, and adding to his income by teaching. Acquired a circle of influential friends, particularly the Von Breuning family, and Count Waldstein.

1792. Haydn passed through Bonn on way home from London. Met Beethoven, who then followed him to Vienna, where he stayed for the rest of his life. His father died soon after, and his brothers came to Vienna too. Had lessons from Haydn, but found him too easy-going and transferred to other teachers, while still admiring him as a composer. Became immersed in all the activities of this most musical city, with its wealthy, aristocratic, musical patrons, many of whom became his friends. Beethoven frequently dedicated his works to them, but tried not to be too dependent on them, and had no court appointment. Earned his living by playing the piano for the aristocracy—he was a great pianist and improviser; by occasionally giving a public concert; by teaching—largely members of the aristocracy; by publication of his compositions—which brought in little money; and by dedications of his works, for which he was sometimes paid. One of the first musicians not to be in the paid service of either the Church or an aristocrat.

1795. First publications: 3 piano trios, op. 1; and 3 piano sonatas, op. 2, all of which Haydn heard Beethoven play at Prince Lichnowsky's house. Continued to compose sonatas and chamber music, his first string quartets, op. 18, and his first 2 piano concertos. These "first period" works show the influence of Haydn and Mozart, but have occasional fiery and unexpected touches that presage his later works.

1800. Gave his first public concert, at which he produced his first symphony. Third piano concerto written this year. The second symphony followed two years later. Began to become alarmed at growing deafness. While in the country in 1802 wrote a pathetic account of it in a last testament intended for his brothers, saying how it cut him off from society and from his art. But he emerged with new courage and strength; and the "second period" works which followed show his maturity.

1803. The third, 'Eroica' symphony, op. 55, composed in this year, marks the beginning of this middle period. It continues up to the eighth symphony, composed in 1812, and includes the 'Waldstein' and 'Appassionata' piano sonatas, the 'Rasumovsky' quartets, the 'Archduke' piano trio, the fourth and fifth piano concertos, the violin concerto, and his one opera 'Fidelio', unsuccessfully produced during the Napoleonic occupation of Vienna in 1805. Was given an annuity by three aristocrats in 1809, but the amount did not come up to expectations. During this period became friendly with many women, but never married. Continually moved his lodgings, and enjoyed visits to the country.

1814. 'Fidelio' repeated, this time with success. Congress of

Vienna, 1814–1815, brought concerts, and money into his pocket.

1815. Brother Caspar died, leaving his son Karl in the guardianship of his wife and his brother Ludwig. Perpetual quarrels and law-suits between the guardians resulted in Beethoven having sole charge after 1820. But Karl responded to Uncle's affection with careless, spendthrift and deceitful ways, and was a continual source of trouble. Composed little in these years.

1820. Was now busy composing his great mass in D, which was finished in 1823, as was the ninth, 'Choral', symphony. To these years belong also his last 3 piano sonatas, and his last 5 string quartets. This is his "third" period, sometimes called "the period of prophetic yearning", during which he seemed to be reaching out for something beyond his ken. His use of the voice in the mass and the "choral" symphony exhibits a sense of striving—choral writing did not come easily to him. He experimented with a combination of contrapuntal and harmonic forms, particularly in the piano sonatas and the quartets. His deafness had now shut him in completely upon himself, and in his loneliness he turned to the solace of composition.

1824. The ninth symphony and part of the mass in D performed.

1826. Karl attempted to shoot himself. When convalescing they went together to Ludwig's youngest brother's country house. Returning in the winter, under bad conditions, Beethoven fell ill, and never recovered. Died in March, 1827. Thousands attended the funeral, and Schubert was a torch bearer.

A social rebel, with uncouth ways, who, in his efforts to get money, did not always deal fairly with his publishers. But had noble, generous impulses, and was loved and revered by many. He was very self-critical and continually revised his works. He enlarged the scope of the sonata and the symphony and made them more dramatic. Although he began by writing in the style of Haydn and Mozart, he ended by looking to the future, and may be called the first "Romantic".

Nine symphonies, including the 'Eroica' (the third), the fifth in C minor, the 'Pastoral' (the sixth), and the 'Choral' (the ninth). 5 piano concertos, including the 'Emperor'; 1 violin concerto; 1 triple concerto for piano, violin and 'cello.

Overtures: 4 for the opera 'Fidelio'—'Leonora 1', '2', and '3' and 'Fidelio'; 'Coriolanus'; 'Egmont'.

32 piano sonatas, including the 'Pathétique', the 'Pastoral', the 'Moonlight', the 'Waldstein', the 'Appassionata', 'Les Adieux', the 'Hammerklavier'. Several sets of piano variations. Bagatelles.

Much chamber music: 16 string quartets, including the 3 'Rasumovsky'; 9 piano trios, including the 'Archduke'; 10 violin and piano sonatas, including the 'Kreutzer'; 5 'cello and piano sonatas; various works for wind combinations; etc.

One opera 'Fidelio' and some incidental music.

Various choral works, the only really great one being the mass in D major. A large number of songs—not his best work. Canons.

Biography and Chief Works of Franz Schubert

1797. Born in Vienna, the son of a schoolmaster. Musical family. Early taught to play the violin and piano.

1808. Good singing voice secured him a place in the Vienna choir school. Quickly became leader of the school's orchestra, and even conducted it occasionally. Thus came in contact with music of Haydn and Mozart and early Beethoven. Early compositions include string quartets for the family to play when at home in the holidays, and his first symphony.

1813. Left choir school and entered a training school for teachers, preparatory to becoming a teacher in his father's school in 1814.

1814. Began to write his first great songs—'Gretchen at the Spinning Wheel', 'The Shepherd's Lament', both settings of Goethe. Found teaching irksome.

1815. Wrote second and third symphonies, 2 piano sonatas, a string quartet, 2 masses, incidental music to 5 plays, and about 145 songs, including 'Hedge Rose', 'Restless Love' and 'The Erl King', all while acting as a schoolmaster!

1816. Gave up teaching, and went to live with a friend in Vienna. Began to have musical evenings at the house of his friends—a new "middle class" growth of music making. Composed the fourth and fifth symphonies, many more songs, including 'Death and the Maiden' and 'The Trout', another string quartet, etc.

1817. Returned to teaching in his father's school for a year, but felt thwarted; his compositions less good.

1818. Appointed music master to Prince Esterhazy's children, in Hungary. Had freedom to compose, but lacked stimulus of musical friendships. Returned to Vienna same year, and lived with a poet. Never returned to school teaching.

1819. Spent a happy three months in the country, during which he composed the 'Trout' quintet. Returned to Vienna, where he lived for the rest of his life, with various friends and relations in turn.

1821. His first songs published, by private subscription. Wrote the opera 'Alfonso and Estrella'.

1822. Wrote first two movements of 'Unfinished' symphony, after which, as with the unfinished 'Quartettsatz', he lost all interest in it. Serious illness. Ailing for the rest of his life.

1823. 'The Maid of the Mill' song cycle. Incidental music to 'Rosamunde'.

1824. Quartets in A minor, and the 'Death and the Maiden'. Octet. Reputation growing in Vienna.

1827. Song cycle 'Winter Journey'. 2 piano trios, piano impromptus. Visited Beethoven on his death bed.

1828. 'Great' symphony in C major. Took greater pains over it than usual. Died of typhoid.

Lived an irregular Bohemian life, among poets and other artistic friends. A gentle, dreamy, easy-going person; much loved. Composed easily and hurriedly, rarely revising a work. The first great *Lieder* writer (see p. 99). His chamber music and symphonies also full of lovely song-like melodies, but sometimes have formal weaknesses, such as too much repetition. Delightful and unusual modulations: particularly fond of modulating from major to tonic minor and vice-versa, and to the key a major third below the tonic. Fond of chromatic harmony.

600 songs, including 3 cycles, 'The Maid of the Mill', 'Winter Journey' and 'Swan Song'. Other famous songs mentioned in biography above.

Much delightful chamber music: 15 string quartets, including 'Death and the Maiden'; 3 piano trios; the 'Trout' quintet for violin, viola, 'cello, double bass and piano; the octet for clarinet, horn, bassoon, 2 violins, 'cello and double bass.

11 symphonies—unequal works. No. 5 in B♭ major, the 'Unfinished' in B minor, and the 'Great' C major are the best known.

Many works for piano solo: 22 sonatas; 8 impromptus; 6 moments musicaux; many waltzes and ländler. Also piano duets.

Much theatre music: operas, including 'Alfonso and Estrella'; incidental music to plays, including 'Rosamunde'. But all suffer from poor librettos, and are theatrically lifeless, though there are touches of Schubertian greatness here and there in the music. Few have been performed, in his lifetime or since.

Church music, including masses; choral works with orchestra, with piano, and unaccompanied. Not much performed today, except the 23rd psalm for female voices and piano, and the mass in G.

Romantics

Chapter Seventeen

The Early Romantics

New movements in music were stirring in the first half of the nineteenth century, and it is customary to call the composers who reached maturity at that time "The Early Romantics".

Romanticism is a word of which everyone is more or less conscious of the meaning, but is quite difficult to define. One good definition is "the blending of strangeness with beauty". Romanticism stresses the imaginative and the visionary rather than the formal, classical aspect of art—poetry rather than pattern. The French Revolution did much to produce explosive forces which had an emotional effect on the arts. Men such as Byron, Shelley, Keats and Wordsworth show the romantic element in English poetry. Interest in nature and in the supernatural grew in all the arts; and the nationalistic element began to come to the fore.

The romantic composers reacted away from the excessive preoccupation with the formal conventions of the lesser classical contemporaries of Mozart and Beethoven. And perhaps, too, they unconsciously felt that they could not write better symphonies than Mozart and Beethoven themselves, and wished to experiment in other mediums. They tended to take more interest in literature than the earlier composers had done, and it often affected their music. We find some of them writing symphonic poems, with a programmatic basis, instead of symphonies; others developing the poetic tonal possibilities of the piano; and they were often more interested in writing short pieces in free forms, with titles, than large formal structures, with mere opus numbers.

The Growth of Piano Writing

The first distinctively pianistic writing appeared at this time. Beethoven, in spite of all the beauty of his piano sonatas, hardly realised the tonal possibilities of the pianistic idioms that Chopin and Schumann discovered soon afterwards. His sonatas are more like symphonies in miniature, and could well be arranged for the orchestra, whereas a Chopin nocturne is unthinkable in any other medium. There is an undoubted romantic element in Beethoven's later writings, more particularly in his harmonies and his dynamics, and he has sometimes been called the "first romantic"; but on the whole, the classical element in his music is predominant. This also applies to the piano music of Schubert, who keeps to the traditional forms in his piano writing much more than in his songs.

Weber was a contemporary of Beethoven and Schubert, but he comes into this, rather than the last, chapter, because he was not Viennese, and his contribution to German opera is definitely romantic. He wrote a good deal of piano music, though it is not often played today. It is very pianistic, though sometimes rather weak in form. He wrote a number of sonatas, two polonaises, a well-known 'Rondo Brillante, and an 'Invitation to the Dance'.

Chopin has been called the poet of the piano. He realised to the full the possibilities inherent in the use of the pedal, and his accompanying figuration is very pianistic. He wrote nothing of any importance except piano music. His works are listed after his biography on p. 159.

Schumann, too, developed a distinctive piano style, though, unlike Chopin, he was interested in other mediums. He experimented with pedal effects, as, for instance, at the end of 'Papillons'. His harmonies are warm, rich and colourful, and he was fond of cross rhythms. He wrote 3 piano sonatas, in addition to a large number of shorter pieces, which are listed under his name on p. 161. 'Carnaval', which is largely programme music, is perhaps the best known and is a collection of short pieces, loosely held together by a "programme".

Mendelssohn's piano music, more particularly his 'Songs without Words', was exceedingly popular at the time it was written, and was much played in Victorian drawing-rooms. But it has worn rather thin, and does not represent the best side of his work. A few pieces, such as his 6 preludes and fugues, his brilliant 'Andante and Rondo Capriccioso', and his 'Variations Sérieuses' rise above the general level. He also wrote a number of organ sonatas.

Liszt (1811–1886) was the most brilliant pianist of his day, and he wrote many very difficult piano pieces that are still popular with pianists who have a brilliant technique and wish to show it off. Musically, most of them have not very much of importance to say, though the B minor sonata is a fine work. He wrote arrangements of many songs and operatic arias for the piano; and his Hungarian dances have great verve.

Programme Music. The Symphonic Poem and the Concert Overture

The most interesting orchestrator of this period was *Berlioz*. He experimented in all kinds of orchestral combinations, and produced effects that had never been heard before. His three so-called symphonies are quite unlike the symphonies of Mozart and Beethoven. The 'Fantastic symphony' has an extraordinary programme based on his own life (see his biography on p. 153); 'Harold in Italy' has a programme based on Byron's 'Childe Harold', and a solo viola part; 'Romeo and Juliet' is again programmatic, and includes solo voices and a chorus. In these works he uses a recurring theme which he calls *l'idée fixe,* to represent one particular person or idea.

Liszt was actually the first person to use the term "programme music", and to write what he called "symphonic poems" (see p. 90). He wrote two programmatic symphonies in several movements, the 'Dante' and the 'Faust' symphonies. But he thought that a continuous one-movement work could express a programme more freely, hence his invention of the symphonic poem. 'Tasso', 'Les

Preludes', and 'Mazeppa' are his best-known works in this medium. He used what he called "metamorphosis of themes", akin to *L'idée fixe* of Berlioz and the *Leitmotiv* of Wagner.

Liszt was a wonderful pianist, a prolific composer of brilliant piano pieces, the inventor of the symphonic poem, an instigator of "the music of the future", and a warm and generous supporter of composers such as Berlioz and Wagner. But he was not himself a really great composer, and, apart from his piano pieces, his music is rarely heard today.

Concert overtures are not unlike symphonic poems, and *Mendelssohn* is considered to be their inventor. His two best-known concert overtures are 'A Midsummer Night's Dream' and 'The Hebrides', but they are both in sonata form, although they are programme music. Later examples of concert overtures are, however, sometimes so free in form that they are indistinguishable from symphonic poems.

The Symphony and the Concerto

While these experiments in programme music were taking place, however, some of the more conservative composers still continued to compose classical symphonies and concertos. *Schumann* wrote 4 symphonies, which just miss greatness because he was not a very good orchestrator and found large forms more difficult to manage than small ones. But his piano concerto is one of the most popular in the present-day repertoire, and his 'cello concerto is played quite frequently.

Mendelssohn wrote 5 symphonies, in addition to a number of youthful ones which have not been published. The best known are the 'Scottish' and the 'Italian'. But in spite of their titles they have very little "programme" and are in classical forms. He also wrote 2 piano concertos which are played occasionally, and a violin concerto which is extremely popular.

Chopin and *Liszt* each wrote 2 piano concertos, but Chopin was not a good orchestrator, and Liszt's concertos are brilliant rather than profound, so none of them are really great works, though they are still occasionally heard.

Chamber Music

There are few chamber works in this period to compare with those of Haydn, Mozart and Beethoven a generation earlier, or Brahms a generation later. *Schumann* and *Mendelssohn* both wrote string quartets, but their best-known chamber works make use of the piano. Schumann's piano quintet is his most frequently played chamber work, but there are also 2 piano quartets, 3 piano trios, and 4 string quartets. Mendelssohn's output is quite large. It includes 2 piano trios, 3 piano quartets and one piano sextet; and 6 quartets, 2 quintets and one octet for strings. Both composers also wrote sonatas for a solo instrument and piano.

The other composers referred to in this chapter were not interested in chamber music. Mendelssohn and Schumann were more conservative, and therefore more interested in the classical forms and chamber music.

Song

Schubert's songs have been referred to in the last chapter. They mark the beginning of the romantic period, as far as song writing is concerned. *Schumann* and *Mendelssohn* followed on, each writing a large number of art songs. Mendelssohn's have mostly worn rather thin, though 'On Wings of Song' is still immensely popular. Schumann's have fared rather better. They have a more interesting accompaniment, with richer harmonies. Songs such as 'Thou bloomest like a Flower', 'Dedication', 'The Two Grenadiers', and the cycles 'Woman's Life and Love' and 'The Poet's Love' should live for some time to come. A few of Liszt's songs are still sung today. The medium did not interest the other great composers of this period.

Opera

Opera continued to be popular throughout the period, and Italian opera was firmly established in all the capitals of Europe. *Rossini* (1792–1868) was the most popular Italian opera composer, and his opera 'The Barber of Seville' is still frequently given today. He was director of the opera house at Naples, and wrote 36 operas in nineteen years. Then, at the age of 37, with the production of 'William Tell', he ceased to write any more, though he lived to the age of 76!

But this was the period when opera began to be regularly written and accepted in other languages too. Following on Mozart's 'Magic Flute' and Beethoven's 'Fidelio' in German, came *Weber*, the first romantic German opera writer. His 'Der Freischütz' is based on a German legend, and is full of romantic colour, as, for example, in the incantation scene, when magic bullets are cast with gruesome spells at midnight. It also contains popular German peasant songs and dances. 'Euryanthe' is a German grand opera and 'Oberon' was written in English for a London performance. Weber intended to produce a German version, but he died before he could do so. Weber laid the foundation of German romantic opera, on which Wagner was later to build.

In France *Berlioz* wrote 3 romantic operas in the French language. 'Benvenuto Cellini' was a failure, though an interlude from it became popular as the overture 'Carnaval Romain'. 'Les Troyens' was so enormous that only half of it was given in his lifetime, while 'Beatrice and Benedict' was a light comic opera that was first produced in Germany. So he made little impact on French opera at the time, and composers like Rossini were much more popular in Paris.

Russia was another country where Italian opera held sway. But in 1836 *Glinka* produced an opera 'A Life for the Czar', which is the first great opera in the Russian language. 'Russlan and Ludmilla' followed, and thenceforward Russian opera became fully established, leading to the works of Borodin, Rimsky Korsakov and Moussorgsky in the second half of the century.

Sacred Music

With the growth of romanticism less interest was taken in sacred music. *Mendelssohn's* is perhaps the best-known today. His greatest oratorio 'Elijah' was composed for Birmingham. It creates a series of pictures of the prophet's life. 'St Paul' and 'The Hymn of Praise' are also quite well known, as are a number of his anthems, such as 'Hear my Prayer'.

Berlioz's 'L'enfance du Christ' is an oratorio which is quite different from his highly romantic orchestral music. It is simple and devout, and quite short, and is frequently performed in France, and occasionally in England.

Biography and Chief Works of Carl Maria von Weber

1786. Born near Lübeck, North Germany. Father a violinist, a member of a family of musicians. (His niece married Mozart.) He toured Europe as a Director of a dramatic company, taking his family with him, so Carl became familiar with the stage.

1796. Family moved to Salzburg. Carl joined the choir school in 1798, under Michael Haydn, brother of Joseph. But family moved again six months later. Mother died. Began to play at concerts and to compose, while continuing to tour.

1803. Had lessons from Abt Vogler (of Browning's poem) in Vienna. Also met Haydn.

1804. Appointed Kapellmeister at Breslau. Conducted at the theatre, and became known as pianist, extemporiser and piano teacher. Also sang to his own guitar accompaniment.

1807. Napoleonic wars made music-making difficult, so became private secretary to a dissolute duke at Stuttgart. Led a gay, frivolous life. Was about to have an opera produced there when he and his father were imprisoned for alleged bribery. Innocence established, but banished from state.

1810. Restless years, always travelling, attracting attention with his romantic personality and his music. Began to write musical criticism. Wrote singspiel 'Abu Hassan'. Met a clarinettist at Munich and wrote 3 concertos for him. Was in Berlin when his father died, leaving him homeless.

1813. Settled at last in Prague as Kapellmeister, becoming an excellent operatic conductor and administrator. Also composed German national songs which appealed to the growing sense of German nationalism.

1816. Appointed Director of new German opera company in Dresden, establishing opera in the vernacular, and collecting together a good body of singers and an orchestra. Some rivalry at first with established Italian opera.

1817. Married one of the Prague opera singers.

1821. 'La Preciosa', a play with music, produced in Berlin. 'Der Freischütz' then followed at a newly-built Berlin opera house for German opera. Created extraordinary patriotic enthusiasm. Was immediately produced by opera houses all over Germany.

1822. Produced Beethoven's 'Fidelio', another German opera, in Dresden.

1823. 'Euryanthe' produced in Vienna. His intention was to produce grand opera in which the dramatic side was more important than it was in Italian opera. But libretto long and confused, performance had to compete with Rossini's highly successful operas, and it was not a success. Performed elsewhere, usually with same disappointing results. Became depressed and ill.

1825. Commissioned to produce an English opera, 'Oberon'. Learnt English in order to do so. Composed music in spite of rapidly failing health.

1826. Arrived in London, and gave selections from 'Der Freischütz' amid great enthusiasm. 'Oberon' splendidly produced. Had agreed to English visit in order to provide money for his family, but though longing for home, he died of tuberculosis, before he could leave London.

A highly romantic figure, who created many friends and several enemies in his short life. Much admired by Germans for his national songs, and his development of German opera. Essentially a dramatic composer; but also a fine pianist and improviser, whose piano compositions were very popular, and are still occasionally played today.

A number of operas, all, except 'Oberon', in the German language. 'Der Freischütz' the best, containing German songs, and a strong romantic and magical element. Laid foundation of German national opera. 'Euryanthe' and, even more, the English 'Oberon' suffer from poor libretti.

Incidental music for many German plays.

Many German national songs.

Many piano pieces, including 4 sonatas, a grand polonaise, 'Rondo Brillante' and 'Invitation to the Dance'.

Three concertos for clarinet and 1 for bassoon. Other orchestral and chamber works relatively unimportant.

Music criticism.

Biography and Chief Works of Hector Berlioz

1803. Born in a small town near Grenoble, in S.E. France. Son of a doctor, who gave him a good education and intended him to be a doctor, too.

1821. Sent to Paris for medical studies, but neglected them and went to hear Gluck's operas instead. Romantic and emotional nature. Gave up medicine and started to study music at Paris Conservatoire, in spite of parental opposition.

1825. Had a mass performed, requiring an orchestra of 150 players.

1827. Competed for Prix de Rome—an annual scholarship entitling the winner to live for four years in Rome, studying and doing creative work. Given for five arts, including music. But failed to obtain it. Heard Irish actress, Henrietta Smithson, in Shakespearean roles, and fell in love with her. Wrote scenes from 'Faust', which he dedicated to her, but she ignored him.

1829–1830. Wrote his 'Fantastic symphony' ("an episode in the life of an artist") in 5 movements, a dream of a poet crossed in love who has taken poison. Everyone in Paris knew it referred to Henrietta Smithson, and was meant to discredit her. He used one theme to represent her throughout, which he called *l'idée fixe*. Highly romantic, the first intrusion of a composer's private life into his work. Successfully performed in Paris.

Obtained Prix de Rome at 5th attempt, and went to Rome.

1832. Returned to Paris, without completing his four years in Rome. The 'Fantastic symphony' given again. Henrietta Smithson invited to the performance. Few days later they met for the first time; they married in 1833, in spite of parental opposition. Had a son, but happiness did not last.

1834. 'Harold in Italy', a programmatic symphony in 4 movements, with a solo viola part, intended for Paganini, who never
played it. Again made use of *l'idée fixe*.

1835. Had already done much journalistic music criticism.
Now appointed permanent music critic to "Journal des
Débats". Continued with music criticism for 30 years.

1837. Requiem composed and performed at a military ceremony,
with hundreds of voices, a large orchestra, and 4 brass bands.
Not a traditional mass, but a terrifying drama.

1838. His first opera 'Benvenuto Cellini' produced in Paris,
amid storms of disapproval. Rarely given since, but an interlude, now called 'Carnaval Romain' is regularly played as a
concert overture.

1839. 'Romeo and Juliet' a "symphony for solo voices, chorus
and orchestra". Contains 'Queen Mab' scherzo. Deserted
his wife in favour of a second-rate singer, and toured Europe
with her. Met Mendelssohn and Wagner.

1844. Published a treatise on orchestration, still of importance
today.

1846. Wrote a "concert opera", 'The Damnation of Faust',
while travelling in Germany and Eastern Europe. Unsuccessful performance in Paris. Never given again in his
lifetime. A gigantic work, of unequal merits. 'Hungarian
March', 'Ballet des Sylphes', and 'The Ride to the Abyss' often
given separately.

1847. Visited Russia, where he made money.

1848. Short period in England, during the 1848 revolution.
Began to write his famous memoirs. Continued to give
concerts in London, Paris and elsewhere.

1854. Wife died. Married his singer. Produced oratorio
'L'enfance du Christ'. Wrote words and music. A small
scale, serene catholic work, very different from his previous
ones.

1860. Extracts from Wagner's operas, and finally 'Tannhauser'
given in Paris. Berlioz unsympathetic. They quarrelled in
print.

1862. 'Beatrice and Benedict', a light opera, given at Baden-
Baden, and later at Weimar. Overture frequently heard
today.

1863. 'The Trojans', an enormous opera, based on Virgil, had occupied Berlioz for many years. Second half 'The Trojans in Carthage' produced at last. First half never produced in his lifetime. Reverts to classical style, using recitatives and arias.

1867. Only son died, leaving him alone.

1869. Died, in Paris.

Chiefly famous for his experiments in orchestration, and for the immensity of his conceptions. His ideal orchestra was 467 players! His writing has many defects of melody, harmony and form, but is redeemed by its freedom of rhythm and its orchestral colour. A pioneer of musical romanticism, his life was equally romantic and violently dramatic. His *l'idée fixe* was the fore-runner of Wagner's *Leitmotiv*. Well known as a music critic and much influenced by literary romantic writers.

Symphonic works: 3 "so called" symphonies, all very irregular, and dependent on a programme: 'Fantastic symphony', 'Harold in Italy'; 'Romeo and Juliet' (with voices).

Operas. 'Benvenuto Cellini'; 'The Trojans'; 'Beatrice and Benedict'. Overtures to the first and last often performed today. Also concert overture 'Carnaval Romain', based on music taken from 'Benvenuto Cellini'.

Many choral works, including 'The Damnation of Faust', the 'Requiem' and the oratorio 'L'enfance du Christ'.

Biography and Chief Works of Felix Mendelssohn

1809. Born in Hamburg of Jewish parents. Father a rich banker, grandfather a famous philosopher. Moved to Berlin in 1811, where the four children were given an excellent education. Became Christians. Fanny (born in 1805) and Felix early showed great musical aptitude. Felix produced many early compositions, played the piano and extemporised. Regular Sunday morning chamber concerts in own home, when famous musicians came to play with the children. Visited Goethe, and impressed him.

1825. Decided on a musical career, after visiting Cherubini in Paris. Family moved to a large mansion in Berlin, with a theatre-concert hall in the garden, where even more opportunities of music making were possible. By 1825 had composed 3 piano quartets, 3 string quartets, a string quintet and the octet.

1826. A reading of Shakespeare's 'A Midsummer Night's Dream' resulted in the concert overture of that name, performed in piano duet and orchestral version.

1827. Went to University, and met more famous people, including German philosophers. A growing enthusiasm for Bach and Handel. Stimulated interest in a revival of their works. Arranged rehearsals of Bach's 'St Matthew Passion' and had it performed in 1829.

1829. Education completed by a three-year "Grand Tour" of Europe. Visited England. 'A Midsummer Night's Dream' overture played. Then Scotland, where conceived 'Hebrides' overture and 'Scotch' symphony. Then Italy—the 'Italian' symphony. Met Chopin and Liszt in Paris. Then London again, where began 'Songs without Words'. Wrote delightful letters to Fanny and others, describing his travels.

1833. Appointed conductor to Lower Rhine Festival at Düsseldorf. Very efficient. Began to compose oratorio 'St Paul'.

1835. Appointed conductor of Gewandhaus concerts in Leipzig, and settled happily there. Made Leipzig the musical centre of Germany. Met Schumann and his wife, and Chopin once more. Brilliant social success. Popularised Bach, and performed Schubert's 'Great' C major symphony.

1837. Married—had five children. Another visit to England. 'St Paul' and other works performed at Birmingham.

1841. King of Prussia, anxious to establish supremacy of Berlin, appointed Mendelssohn his kapellmeister, with instructions to found a music section of a new Academy of Arts. But found Berlin musicians unco-operative. Unhappy. Divided time between Berlin and Leipzig.

1843. Another visit to England, where lionised. Visited Queen Victoria at Buckingham Palace. Inaugurated Leipzig Conservatoire, with Schumann on the staff. Commissioned by King of Prussia to write incidental music to 'A Midsummer Night's Dream'. Began to compose violin concerto.

1846. Produced 'Elijah' at Birmingham. But began to suffer from weariness and depression.

1847. Sister Fanny died. Great shock. Had severe attacks of illness and died in Leipzig. Universally mourned.

A gifted, attractive, versatile, wealthy man who received much adulation. A classical scholar and an athlete. A great conductor and administrator, who popularised Bach and helped to establish great German traditions in music. A fine pianist and organist. Wrote most interesting and attractive letters.

His music sometimes sentimental and superficial, with trite harmony and phrasing, particularly in piano works and songs. But a master of the orchestra, and had great contrapuntal skill. His orchestral and chamber compositions are his best works. He was particularly good at writing music of the Scherzo type. A fine sense of detail. Not a dramatic composer—shrank from exposing his feelings; and in this sense, he was not a typical romantic.

Orchestral works: 5 symphonies, including 'Scotch', 'Italian' and 'Reformation'; 'Concert' overtures to 'A Midsummer Night's Dream' (with incidental music added 16 years later), 'The Hebrides', 'Calm Sea and Prosperous Voyage', 'Melusine', 'Ruy Blas'.

1 violin concerto; 2 piano concertos.

Chamber music: 6 quartets, 2 quintets and octet for strings; 2 piano trios, 3 piano quartets, and 1 piano sextet; 1 violin and 2 'cello sonatas.

Many piano works, some slight, such as the 48 'Songs without Words'; others of more importance, such as the 'Variations Sérieuses', the 6 preludes and fugues, and the 'Andante and Rondo Capriccioso'.

Organ music, including 6 sonatas and 3 preludes and fugues.

Many songs, mostly sentimental and of little value. 'On Wings of Song' the best known. Also vocal duets and unaccompanied part-songs.

Sacred music: a number of anthems, including 'Hear my Prayer'; 'The Hymn of Praise' (a symphonic cantata); and 'Lauda Sion' (a cantata); oratorios, 'St Paul' and 'Elijah.'

Biography and Chief Works of Frédéric Chopin

1810. Born near Warsaw, Poland. Father a Frenchman who went to Poland in 1787, and who became a teacher. Mother a well-educated Pole. Chopin one of four children. Received a good education. Soon playing the piano and composing for it, and performing in homes of aristocracy.

1818. Played a piano concerto at a public concert.

1825. Published his op. 1, a rondo. Interested in Polish folk-music, and began to write mazurkas.

1826. Started a three-year course at Warsaw Conservatoire. Wrote more piano pieces.

1829. Successful concert tour to Vienna. Becoming known in Poland as a national composer. Wrote some Polish pieces, his 2 piano concertos, and some of his studies.

1830. Moved to Vienna with the intention of settling there; but not well received, and only stayed for a year. Heard of capture of Warsaw by Russians, and, in despair, wrote his 'Revolutionary' study.

1831. Moved to Paris, which became his home for the rest of his life. His playing won favourable comment, and his charm made friends at once. Met Berlioz, Liszt, and other famous musicians. A popular piano teacher—preferred teaching to performing in public, but enjoyed playing in the salons of the aristocracy; and soon achieved fame as a composer. Consorted with Polish refugees, and with famous authors who headed the romantic movement.

1834. Travelled through Germany, where he met his parents for the last time. Visited Leipzig, where he met Schumann and Mendelssohn. Became engaged to a Polish girl, but later broke it off, owing to the precarious state of his health.

1837. A visit to England, where he played at the home of Broadwood, the piano manufacturer, but gave no public concerts. On his return to Paris became very friendly with the novelist calling herself George Sand.

1838. George Sand took him to Majorca for his health, together with her two children. But bad weather and primitive conditions brought on tuberculosis. Continued to compose, however. The 24 preludes date from this time.

1839. Continued to live with George Sand, in Paris in the winter, in her country house in the summer. She looked after him well, but his health was precarious. Continued to teach, to compose, and to play for the aristocracy.

1847. Separated from George Sand—her children made difficulties and came between them. Health became worse.

1848. Revolution in Paris. Fled to England. Played in fashionable society, and gave three concerts in London. Concerts also in Manchester, Glasgow and Edinburgh, but desperately ill.

1849. Died in Paris.

Sensitive, cultured, retiring personality. Strong sense of Polish nationality. Founded a new style of piano playing and composing—the poet of the piano. A cantabile style of melody, with delicate or brilliant accompanying ornamentation, creating an atmosphere of its own. His own playing was refined, delicate or fiery, as occasion demanded. Made effective use of the pedal and discreet use of rubato. Wrote a few, not very satisfactory works for piano and orchestra, a few songs, and some miscellaneous compositions. But everything of value is for piano solo. Better at small-scale or fantasia-like works than in larger, formal designs. Wrote Polish dances—mazurkas and polonaises.

Works for piano. Dances: mazurkas; polonaises; waltzes.

Short pieces: preludes; studies; nocturnes (the idea and title taken from the Irish composer Field); impromptus, etc.

Larger works: 4 scherzos; 4 ballades; 3 sonatas, etc.

2 piano concertos, and a few other works for piano and orchestra.

Small quantity of chamber music, and a few Polish songs.

Biography and Chief Works of Robert Schumann

1810. Born, Zwickau in Saxony. Father a bookseller of literary tastes. Browsed in bookshop in early years. Showed equal musical and literary ability. Well educated.

1828. Entered Leipzig university to study law. Met Heine. Attended no lectures, but read the novels of Jean Paul, wrote stories and a few songs. Began piano lessons with Wieck, meeting his daughter, Clara, aged 9, who was already a good pianist.

1829. Transferred to Heidelberg University, but still studied little law. Practised the piano for hours. Impressed by hearing the violinist Paganini. Eventually persuaded his mother (his father being dead) to allow him to study music, instead of law.

1830. Returned to Leipzig, to have piano lessons from Wieck, and to study composition.

1832. Experimented with a contrivance to strengthen the fourth finger, and crippled his right hand. Gave up thoughts of a career as a concert pianist. Went on composing piano pieces.

Much admired Chopin. Went through a period of great depression.

1834. Started a new periodical, dealing with musical criticism, together with Wieck and other friends. Wrote under pen names: Florestan, when feeling fiery; Eusebius, when feeling poetic. Became engaged to Ernestine von Fricken, who lived at Asch. Wrote 'Carnaval', in which the letters ASCH are used.

1835. Became more friendly with Clara Wieck, now 15, and broke engagement to Ernestine. Mendelssohn came to live in Leipzig, and they became friends. Also met Chopin.

1837. Proposed to Clara. Father opposed the marriage. Wrote many of his best piano works about this time.

1838. Moved to Vienna, in the hopes of settling there. But found little scope. Met Schubert's brother, and discovered the MS. of his C major symphony. Returned to Leipzig.

1839. Went to law, to force Wieck to allow him to marry his daughter. Court proceedings dragged on.

1840. Lovers given permission to marry at last. Schumann so happy that he wrote over 100 songs.

1841. Wrote 3 symphonies and the first movement of the piano concerto. Clara played this just before giving birth to the first of her eight children.

1842. A period of chamber music writing—3 string quartets, piano quartet, and piano quintet.

1843. Mendelssohn opened Leipzig conservatoire, and appointed Schumann as professor. But an ineffectual teacher and conductor.

1844. Robert and Clara went on a concert tour to Russia. Clara's playing attracted more attention than his compositions, as always. Settled in Dresden, where they met Wagner. Periods of morbidity. Fewer compositions, though finished another symphony, and made several attempts at writing an opera 'Genoveva', which was finished in 1848. Also wrote 'Album for the Young' for his daughter's birthday. Fled from Dresden during the 1848 revolution, but soon returned.

1850. Made music director at Düsseldorf. Wrote the 'cello concerto, and 'Manfred' overture, and his last symphony, the 'Rhenish'. But again unsuccessful, socially and as a conductor. Showed more signs of mental illness.

1853. Met Brahms, aged 20. Wrote of him "This is he that should come". Conducting had become so bad that was asked to resign.

1854. Became mentally deranged, and threw himself into the Rhine. Rescued and taken to an asylum. Brahms went to see him there, but never allowed to see his wife until two days before his death in 1856.

A dreamy, moody, emotional personality, with nervous disorders and insanity in the family. A disciple of the writer, Jean Paul—much of his music has literary ideas behind it. Always composed at the piano—a means of emotional self-expression. Mainly a piano composer until 1840; short pieces showing a lyrical quality, a richness of harmony and emotional warmth. Fond of cross rhythms and syncopation. Very romantic style. Great spurt of song writing in year of marriage. Songs had important piano part, with melody often shared between voice and piano. A year of orchestral compositions followed, and then a year of chamber music. Later compositions less good on the whole, as insanity crept upon him. Better at writing miniatures than large-scale works. Not good at creating ideas capable of development. Orchestration too heavy—doubled wind parts for safety, because his conducting was unreliable. Choral writing rather poor. A good writer of music criticism.

Large amount of piano music, including 'Carnaval', 'Papillons'; 'Études Symphoniques'; 'Kreisleriana'; 3 sonatas; 'Novelletten'; 'Album for the Young', etc.

Large number of songs, many written in 1840, including the cycles 'Myrtles'; 'Woman's Life and Love'; 'Poet's Love'. Also part songs.

Chamber music, including piano quintet, 2 piano quartets, 3 piano trios, 3 violin sonatas, 3 string quartets.

4 symphonies; 1 piano concerto; 1 'cello concerto; overtures to 'Manfred', 'Faust', etc.

Opera 'Genoveva'; incidental music to 'Manfred'; a number of choral works with orchestra—all rarely performed today. Not his best work.

Chapter Eighteen

The Second Half of the Nineteenth Century

The giants of this period were Brahms and Wagner. Brahms wrote "absolute" music in the classical tradition, although his compositions have also a lyrical romantic quality. His example was followed by Dvořák and other composers. Wagner revolted against the classical traditions. He was a neo-romantic, who followed the programmatic ideas of Berlioz and Liszt, and who thought that the highest art was a combination of all the arts in the form of "music drama". Pro-Brahms and anti-Wagner feelings ran very high, as did also the opposite, and it appeared, at the time, to be almost impossible to appreciate the music of the two, though we can assimilate and enjoy both today. There was also a strong growth of nationalistic tendencies, as evidenced particularly in Russia and Czecho-Slovakia.

Nationalist Composers

European musical composition up to the end of the eighteenth century had been largely cosmopolitan and international. But racial and national characteristics had always been present in the folk dances and songs of the people; and, with the awakening of patriotic nationalisms in the nineteenth century, came a consciousness of the national idioms and characteristics in folk music which could be applied to other kinds of music.

The German nationalistic spirit arose first, and showed in Weber's operas and in Schumann's interest in German literature. Then Chopin began to write Polish national dances and Liszt his Hungarian dances.

But the first really strong growth of nationalistic musical feeling arose in Russia in the second half of the nineteenth century. Round about 1860 a group of Russian composers, who called themselves "the five", met together with the aim of establishing a specifically Russian style of music, taking Glinka (who was mentioned on p. 150) as their forerunner and example. Balakirev was the only one who was trained in youth as a professional musician, and he acted as adviser and mentor to the other four. Cui was an army officer, Borodin a famous chemist, Moussorgsky a civil servant, and Rimsky-Korsakov a naval officer, though he began to study music seriously later in life, and then taught at the St Petersburg Conservatoire. They did not want to be influenced by German and Italian traditions, but based their music on Russian folk tunes and legends, on Russian church music and oriental idioms. They tended to despise academic training, and they freely helped each other, even to the extent of finishing or improving each other's compositions.

Balakirev (1837–1910), though a fluent composer, was not a great one, and little of his music is played today. The same applies to *Cui* (1835–1918). But *Borodin* (1833–1887) wrote a number of works of great value, including a fine symphony, 2 string quartets, a tone poem 'In the Steppes of Central Asia', and, perhaps greatest of all, his opera 'Prince Igor'.

Moussorgsky (1839–1881) was the most original of the five, though his greatest work, the opera 'Boris Godounov', was almost completely rewritten after his death by Rimsky-Korsakov, who did not understand his original idioms, and smoothed out what he thought were its crudities. It was not until 1928 that Moussorgsky's original score was published and was seen to be far superior. Rimsky-Korsakov also completed Moussorgsky's unfinished tone poem 'A Night on the Bare Mountain'. Moussorgsky's fine songs were relatively unknown until some time after his death. 'The Song of the Flea' is now very popular. His 'Pictures from an Exhibition' was written for the piano, but is best known today in an orchestrated version by the Frenchman Ravel.

Rimsky-Korsakov (1844–1908) was a skilful and colourful orchestrator, and his tone poem 'Scheherazade', the story of the Arabian Nights, is a very popular work. 'Ivan the Terrible' is a dramatic opera and 'Le Coq d'Or' is a fantastic, fairy-tale one, but both are full of barbaric oriental colour.

Tschaikowsky (1840–1893) is the best known of the Russian composers of this period, but, unlike the five, he studied at a conservatoire and was influenced by the Germanic traditions of the Rubinstein brothers. Consequently he was always rather suspected by the Russian Nationalists. But his music reached Western Europe before theirs did. Although he does not make use of Russian folk song and oriental idioms in the way that they do, he has many Russian qualities, such as his intense emotionalism and his love of contrasts of colour. *Glazounov* (1865–1936), *Scriabin* (1872–1915) and *Rachmaninov* (1873–1943), whose fine piano concerto in C minor and preludes for the piano are so popular, are other Russian composers who lived a generation later.

The cult of Nationalism spread rapidly from Russia to other countries. *Smetana* (1824–1884) was a musician in Bohemia (or Czecho-Slovakia, as it is called today) at a time when it was ruled by Austria. In 1862 the Czechs were given a greater measure of freedom and allowed to establish their own opera house in Prague. Smetana was soon made its conductor, and he began to write operas in the Czech language, the best known of which is 'The Bartered Bride'. He soon became the champion of Czech music, and it was said that "his works are the best medium for the Czech to become conscious of his national character". He also wrote a set of 6 symphonic poems called 'My Fatherland'. He prepared the way for *Dvořák*, who was very conscious of his Czech nationality and Slavonic race.

Grieg (1843–1907) was a Norwegian who received his musical training in Leipzig, but who began to make use of national folk music and legends, and consciously to develop Norwegian national music.

By the turn of the century nationalism in music had spread to Finland, Spain, Hungary and Britain, but that is a matter for the next chapter.

Opera

In opera, the most important figure in the nineteenth century was undoubtedly *Wagner*. As a boy he had great admiration for Beethoven, who, he later declared, was reaching out in his ninth symphony for the consummation of music and words which he himself set out to achieve in "music drama".

He was also much influenced by the operatic aims of Gluck, and by the German nationalism shown in Weber's operas. Wagner made much use of German myths and legends. He glorified the "nordic" element; and in the twentieth century his music became closely linked with the ideals of Hitler and the Nazis, and was received with great enthusiasm in Germany.

Wagner believed that the art work of the future was to be a fusion of all the arts of the theatre: music, poetry, acting, dancing, stage setting; and he attempted to achieve this unity in himself. He wrote his own libretti, and tried to direct, in detail, the performances of his operas. He even designed and helped to build his theatre at Bayreuth.

He wanted a fellowship of all the artists (though he himself was a most quarrelsome individual!), and he wanted the public to take art seriously and to attend a festival almost as a sacred duty, as at Bayreuth.

He gradually created a free "arioso" style of melody, which was in speech rhythm (like recitative), and yet was musical and song-like (as in aria). But he avoided the set song, as being undramatic. In place of regular form, as for example ternary form, he got unity by using *Leitmotive* to illustrate persons or ideas or moods, and combined them very freely.

He used a much larger orchestra than most operatic composers, and made much use of brass. If he wanted a certain type of instrument that did not exist, he invented it. The orchestra was not merely an accompaniment, it was an integral part of the texture, and often commented effectually on the story by means of *Leitmotive*, while the singers were silent. (For example, the "curse" motiv is used when the ring is passed from one person to another in 'The Ring', though the persons on the stage do not know it is cursed.)

The theatre at Bayreuth was designed by Wagner. The auditorium was fan-shaped, and the orchestra was sunken, so that the conductor would not distract the audience. This meant also that the singers could more easily get their voices over the large orchestral tone volume. The most elaborate scenery, machinery and lighting were used. When 'Parsifal' was written, its performance was confined to Bayreuth for twenty years, so that it could be performed in just the way the composer wanted.

Wagner's greatest achievements were his wonderful power of music development and his mastery of the orchestra. He is as great as Beethoven in his power of developing and combining germs of musical thought and working them up to a climax; and his orchestration had a great effect on all the next generation of composers, though no one (except the lesser composer Humperdinck, who wrote 'Hansel and Gretel') followed on his footsteps in writing his kind of "music drama". Much of Wagner's music is capable of being transferred to the concert room, and some people even consider that he would have made a greater symphonist than an operatic composer.

But side by side with this great rise of Wagnerian music drama, Italian opera continued to be performed in every large music centre in Europe. *Donizetti*, *Bellini*, and, later, *Puccini*, were three of the best-known composers, but *Verdi* (1813–1901) was the greatest of them all. He had written 16 operas, all of which had been successfully produced in various towns in Italy, before he wrote his first 3 operas which are still in the regular repertoire: 'Rigoletto', 'Il Trovatore' and 'La Traviata'. These, written between 1851 and 1853, are, like the earlier operas, in the typical Italian style, but they are more mature, more full of bold characterisation, dramatic situations and lyrical melodies.

Between 1853 and 1867 Verdi wrote or rewrote 7 operas, of which 'Un Ballo in Maschera' is the best known. Then, in 1870, he accepted a commission to write 'Aida' for a newly-opened opera house in Cairo. This is a spectacular opera, using a large chorus and ballet, though it is still full of Italianate melody. But the orchestral part is fuller and more harmonically interesting than in any of his earlier operas.

When Verdi was 74, he wrote a serious dramatic opera, 'Otello', that used *Leitmotive*, and had obviously been influenced by the operas of Wagner. Even more surprising, at 80 he wrote a light-hearted comic opera, 'Falstaff', that was again Wagnerian in style and scope, and bears comparison with Wagner's 'Mastersingers'. But in both these works the emphasis is still on the voices. He always gives them good melodies, and he never swamps them, as Wagner tends to do.

In France, *Gounod* wrote two popular operas, 'Faust' and 'Romeo and Juliet'; and *Bizet* completed 'Carmen' only a month or so before his early death in 1875.

Three of the greatest Russian operas, after Glinka had shown the way, were *Borodin's* 'Prince Igor', *Moussorgsky's* 'Boris Godounov', and *Rimsky-Korsakov's* 'Ivan the Terrible', though the latter's 'Coq d'Or' is better known in this country. They are all very Russian in style and feeling, with strong, barbaric, oriental colouring. Opera has been very popular in Russia ever since, as has also the ballet, in which Russia developed a distinctive style.

Smetana and *Dvořák* wrote many Czech operas, though Smetana's 'The Bartered Bride' is the only one that is regularly performed in this country. It is a comedy about Czech village life, and is full of gay peasant dances and songs.

Orchestral Music

Brahms's first symphony was hailed by enthusiastic supporters as "the tenth", thus declaring what is generally accepted today, that it was the greatest since Beethoven's nine. His four magnificent symphonies follow on the great Viennese classical tradition. Brahms was able to build large-scale works in a way that had been beyond the ability

of the earlier romantics, and his powers of organic development were as great as those of Beethoven.   But there is also
a lyrical warmth in his melodies that shows the influence of
romanticism.

Dvořák owed much to Brahms, and his 'New World'
symphony and the fourth symphony in G major are very
popular today.   They are tuneful and skilfully orchestrated
works, though sometimes a little weak organically.

Tschaikowsky's symphonies are also very popular, particularly the fourth, fifth and sixth (the 'Pathetic').   They,
too, are tuneful and skilfully orchestrated, but they have a
passionate and often melancholy quality that is missing
from Dvořák's sunnier works.

Another very popular symphony belonging to this period
is the one in D minor by the Belgian composer *César Franck*
(1822–1890).   This was written when he was 66, and is his
only symphony.   Franck settled in Paris, and was a comparatively obscure organist, though he gathered a devoted
band of pupils round him.   Most of his music that is of
any value was written after the age of 50, and it received
little recognition during his lifetime.   In addition to the
symphony, he wrote a set of symphonic variations for piano
and orchestra, a fine string quartet, a violin sonata, a few
piano pieces, of which the 'Prelude, Chorale and Fugue' is
the best known, an oratorio 'Les Béatitudes', and a number
of organ works.   There is a strong mystical element throughout his writing, and he is very fond of chromaticisms.

Symphonies were also written by the Russians *Borodin* and
Glazounov (1865–1936), and by the Austrians *Bruckner* (1824–
1896) and *Mahler* (1860–1911).

During this period, *Brahms* and *Tschaikowsky* each wrote
a violin concerto and two piano concertos, while *Grieg's* piano
concerto and *Dvořák's* 'cello and violin concertos are also
popular.

But there was also a wealth of programmatic orchestral
music, so much that it is impossible to mention it all here.
Works of the concert overture or tone-poem type were
written by *Borodin* ('In the Steppes of Central Asia'),
Moussorgsky ('A Night on the Bare Mountain'); *Rimsky-*

Korsakov ('Scheherezade'); *Tschaikowsky* ('Romeo and Juliet', and 'Francesca da Rimini'); *Smetana* ('My Fatherland'); *Dvořák* ('Carnival'); and others.

Chamber Music

Brahms is the greatest exponent in this period. But *Dvořák* wrote some lovely chamber music, too; *Borodin's* two string quartets are often played; *Franck's* violin sonata and string quartet are popular; and *Grieg's* 3 violin sonatas are occasionally heard.

Piano Music and Song

Brahms wrote much lovely piano music. His early piano solos tend to be long and technically very difficult, while his later ones are shorter and often of a poetic, reflective nature. *Moussorgsky's* 'Pictures from an Exhibition', which was later orchestrated by Ravel, is often played in its original piano version, and *Franck's* 'Prelude, Chorale and Fugue', and 'Prelude, Aria and Finale' are two large, cyclic works in which themes from one movement are used in another. Grieg's piano music is slighter, and much of it is playable by the average amateur.

Brahms again heads the list as a song writer, with his hundreds of songs of all types, ranging from his well-known children's songs and arrangements of folk songs to his poetic settings of 'To a Nightingale', 'In Summer Fields' and 'Faint and fainter is my Slumber'. Another great German Lieder writer of this period is *Hugo Wolf*. His many finely constructed songs are romantically imaginative, and very difficult both to play and sing. Although he wrote other works, he is known solely as a song writer. *Moussorgsky*, *Dvořák* and *Grieg* also wrote a number of fine songs, in most cases characteristic of their native country.

Sacred Music

Music had become so secularised by this time that there are comparatively few great sacred works. *Brahms's*

'Requiem' heads the list, with *Verdi's* 'Requiem' a close second. But the two works are quite different, because Brahms's Requiem uses texts from the bible and is an austere work, while Verdi's is a Roman Catholic Requiem, and is rather theatrical in style, though it is undoubtedly deeply felt. *Franck's* oratorio 'Les Béatitudes', *Fauré's* 'Requiem' and *Dvořák's* 'Stabat Mater' are also quite well known.

Biography and Chief Works of Richard Wagner

1813. Born in Leipzig, ninth child of clerk to City Police Courts. Father died same year. Mother married Geyer, an actor, the following year, and moved to Dresden, where Geyer was a member of the Royal Court players. A good stepfather. Richard brought up in atmosphere of theatre. But Geyer died in 1821.

1822. Went to school in Dresden. Interested in literature and studied Greek with enthusiasm. Wrote a tragedy. Also played the piano, and had patriotic admiration for Weber, whom he met.

1827. Returned to Leipzig. Often played truant from school. Sisters on the stage. Heard Beethoven's 'Fidelio' and ninth symphony, both of which made a great impression on him. Began to study harmony and to compose. Also interested in revolutionary political ideas.

1831. Went to Leipzig university, to study music, art and aesthetics. Had first compositions published. Symphony in C major performed.

1833. First appointment, as chorus master at Würzburg opera house, getting valuable theatrical experience. Wrote two operas. Held a series of similar posts at Magdeburg, Königsberg and Riga.

1836. Married Minna, but they had frequent quarrels, culminating in separation in 1862. Began to write 'Rienzi'.

1839. Sailed for London, en route for Paris. Stormy voyage took 3½ weeks. Thought of legend of 'Flying Dutchman'. Crossed to France. Meyerbeer, the operatic composer, befriended him. Three years of struggle and disappointment in Paris. Completed 'Rienzi', the 'Faust' overture, and the libretto of 'The Flying Dutchman'. Began to think about

'Tannhäuser' and 'Lohengrin'. But nothing got performed.
Was impressed by Berlioz's music.

1841. 'Rienzi' accepted in Dresden, and 'The Flying Dutchman' in Berlin—the turn of his fortunes.

1842. Became conductor of Dresden opera. 'Rienzi' successfully produced. 'The Flying Dutchman' given only four
performances in Dresden, but both operas began to be performed elsewhere. Wrote and produced 'Tannhäuser' in
1845, and conducted Beethoven's ninth symphony in 1846.
Wrote 'Lohengrin' in 1847. Continual pecuniary troubles.
Gradually becoming a political agitator.

1849. Took a large share in an abortive revolution. Warrant
issued for his arrest. Fled to Liszt in Weimar; then on to
Switzerland with a false passport. Period of first exile. Made
Zürich his headquarters and began to write books on his
theories of opera and drama. Also wrote an article against
Jews, attacking Meyerbeer who had befriended him.

Liszt performed 'Lohengrin' in Weimar in 1850, and began
a Wagner movement in Germany. But Wagner himself could
not attend performances, as he would have been arrested.
Wrote libretto of 'The Ring' and began the music for it.
Conducted concerts in Zürich. A Wagner festival was held
there in 1853. Paid several visits to Paris, where he met Liszt's
daughter Cosima, then aged 16. Visited London in 1855,
where his music was fiercely condemned by critics, but
applauded by public. A love affair stimulated his writing of
'Tristan and Isolde'.

1858. Moved to Venice, but after some months there, police
asked him to leave, because of his political reputation.

1859. Moved to Paris. Lost money on concerts he gave. Grand
performance of revised 'Tannhäuser' in 1861 proved a fiasco
after 164 rehearsals, costing £8,000. Intense feelings for and
against his music.

1861. Allowed at last to return to Germany. Went to Vienna,
where 'Lohengrin' and 'The Flying Dutchman' given most
successful performances. Performance of 'Tristan and Isolde'
also promised, but continually postponed. Returned to Paris
and wrote libretto of 'The Mastersingers'. Travelled widely,
giving concerts, but always in debt, and being continually
frustrated in getting performances of his operas. His fortunes
at a very low ebb.

1864. Ludwig II, aged 18, acceded to the throne of Bavaria. A Wagner worshipper. Immediately sent for Wagner, gave him a pension and a house, and offered facilities for performances in Munich. Cosima Liszt, who had married Wagner's friend, the conductor Von Bülow, in 1857, came to live with him. 'Tristan' performed in 1865; but cabals formed against him, on account of the King's favouritism, and on the score of extravagance. Finally Ludwig forced to ask him to leave Munich.

1865. Second exile in Switzerland. Settled with Cosima near Lucerne, where stayed for six years. Completed 'Mastersingers', 'Siegfried', and most of 'The Twilight of the Gods', and wrote further prose works. Cosima gave Wagner three children, two girls and a boy, Siegfried, born in 1869. 'The Siegfried Idyll' was performed outside Cosima's bedroom on her birthday, as a tribute in 1870.

Ludwig, in spite of his disapproval of Cosima, continued to support him artistically. 'The Mastersingers' performed in Munich in 1869, and 'The Valkyrie' in 1870.

1871. Wagner Societies formed throughout Europe to raise funds for the erection of a Wagnerian opera house at Bayreuth. The municipality gave the site, and Wagner went to live there in 1872, to superintend the erection. Sunken orchestra of 114 players. Seats for 1,500. Ludwig also gave his support, and built a house for them, "Villa Wahnfried".

1876. First festival held at Bayreuth. 'The Ring' performed in its entirety. Began to compose 'Parsifal'. Performed there in 1882—not allowed to be performed elsewhere for 20 years. Ill health made him spend much of his time in Italy.

1883. Died in Venice. Interred with much ceremony at Bayreuth. His wife continued to direct at Bayreuth, and lived till 1930.

A notorious character, with a fiery eye and a dramatic but charming personality. Loved luxurious living, and had many love affairs. An ardent republican and anti-cleric. Was aggressively sure of his own genius, even when everything went against him. Wrote many ponderous volumes on "the art work of the future", of which he was convinced he was the prophet. Influenced by Beethoven, Weber and Gluck.

Although he wrote a number of other works, it is only his "music dramas" (as he preferred to call his operas) that have lived. He wrote the librettos of them all, in addition to the music. They are very long, and require large-scale production. The texture is so symphonic that extracts from them are often performed in the concert hall.

Music dramas: 'Rienzi'; 'The Flying Dutchman'; 'Tannhäuser'; 'Lohengrin'; 'The Ring' (comprising 'The Rhinegold', 'The Valkyrie', 'Siegfried', and 'The Twilight of the Gods'); 'Tristan and Isolde'; 'The Mastersingers'; and 'Parsifal'. Also a few early operas that are never performed.

Orchestral works: 'The Siegfried Idyll'; 'Faust' overture; 'Symphony in C major'; and some others which are rarely performed.

A few unimportant choral works, piano pieces and songs.

Biography and Chief Works of Johannes Brahms

1833. Born in Hamburg. Father a double bass player. Studied piano and theory, and played in taverns in order to earn money.

1853. Went on a concert tour with a Hungarian violinist. Through this met the famous violinist, Joachim, and Liszt. Visited the Schumanns, who befriended him. Robert Schumann wrote an article in praise of his compositions, and helped him to publish his 3 piano sonatas and some songs.

1854–1856. Stayed in Düsseldorf, helping Clara Schumann and her children while Robert was in the mental asylum. Devoted to Clara throughout his life. Schumann's death made Brahms think of writing a requiem.

1857. Returned to Hamburg, but also held part-time post as music director at the court of Detmold for three years. Started to write a symphony, but turned first two movements of it into piano concerto in D minor, which was performed in Leipzig in 1859. Also wrote two orchestral serenades. Conducted a ladies' choir in Hamburg, for which he wrote part songs. Wrote a manifesto with Joachim against the "Neo-German" school of Wagner and Liszt. Preferred the traditional forms, and wrote much chamber music at this time.

1863. Moved to Vienna, after a disappointment at not being given a conducting post in Hamburg the previous year. Stayed there for the rest of his life. Was conductor of the "Singakadamie" for a year. Continued to write chamber music.

1865. Mother's death gave him the impulse to complete the 'Requiem', which was given a successful performance in Bremen Cathedral, and soon regularly performed in Germany. Wrote 3 more choral works, including 'Alto Rhapsody'.

1872. Appointed a musical director in Vienna, but resigned three years later, and thereafter held no public appointment.

1873. 'St Antony Variations'.

1876. Completed first symphony in C minor. Joachim conducted it in England the following year.

1877. Second symphony in D major.

1878. Violin concerto. Conducted second symphony in home town of Hamburg.

1879. Offered doctorate at Breslau University, and wrote 'Academic Festival Overture' for the occasion. Von Bülow left Wagner, befriended Brahms, and became a famous conductor of his works.

1881. Second piano concerto in B♭ major.

1883. Third symphony in F major.

1885. Fourth symphony in E minor.

1887. Concerto for violin and 'cello.

1889. Honorary freedom of Hamburg.

1891. Clarinettist encouraged him to write clarinet trio and quintet, and, in 1894, 2 clarinet sonatas. Later piano compositions date from this period.

1896. Clara Schumann died—a great blow.

1897. Died in Vienna, Dvořák being a pall-bearer at his funeral.

Lived a quiet uneventful life, and never married. Warmhearted, and had many friends, in spite of awkward, rugged manners.

His music has a warm, romantic, lyrical quality, but he wrote absolute rather than programme music, and followed on the tradition of the classicists. Like Beethoven, he had great powers of thematic development, and was at his best in chamber and orchestral music. But he also followed the Viennese tradition created by Schubert in writing a magnificent collection of songs.

Orchestral works: 4 symphonies; 2 serenades; 'Variations on a theme of Haydn' ('St Antony Variations'); 2 piano concertos; violin concerto; concerto for violin and 'cello; 'Academic Festival Overture'; 'Tragic Overture'; Hungarian Dances.

Large amount of chamber music, including 3 string quartets; 2 string quintets; 2 string sextets; 3 piano trios; 3 piano quartets; 1 piano quintet; 3 violin sonatas; 2 'cello sonatas; 2 clarinet sonatas; horn trio; clarinet trio; and clarinet quintet.

Many works for piano solo: 3 sonatas; 4 ballades; several sets of variations, including those on a theme of Paganini—all early works. Later works are shorter and have indeterminate titles, such as rhapsody, capriccio and intermezzo.

'Liebeslieder' waltzes and Hungarian dances for piano duet. (The waltzes also have optional parts for vocal quartet.)

Organ works, including 11 chorale preludes.

Choral works, including Requiem, 'Alto Rhapsody', part songs for female voices, unaccompanied part songs and motets.

About 200 songs, many of them very beautiful. Also many arrangements of folk songs.

Biography and Chief Works of Alexander Borodin

1833. Born in St Petersburg (now Leningrad). Father a Prince. Brought up by mother. Given good education at home, and learnt German, French, English and Italian. Equally interested and gifted in science and music.

1850. Went to medical school. Particularly interested in chemistry; but continued to enjoy music and to compose it in his spare time.

1856. Finished medical course and served in a military hospital. Met Moussorgsky.

1859. Sent to Western Europe to study chemistry.

1861. Met a Russian pianist in Germany, and fell in love with her. Heard Wagner operas together. They went on to Italy, where he continued to study chemistry and to compose music in his spare time.

1862. Appointed professor of chemistry in St Petersburg, where he continued to work as a chemist for the rest of his life. Married the pianist, and was very happy with her.

Met Balakirev, who made him aware of his Russian musical heritage, and stimulated him to compose his first symphony in E♭. Finished in 1867 and performed in 1868. Became one of "the five". From now onwards followed both professions.

1869. Adopted a 7-year-old girl. Began a second symphony in

B minor, and the opera 'Prince Igor'. Helped to found
medical school for women.

1877. Second symphony performed, after re-orchestrating two
movements of which he had lost the score. Went to visit
laboratories in Germany, and met Liszt. 'Prince Igor' still
unfinished, and was left entirely untouched from 1881 to 1886.

1880. Liszt arranged performance of E♭ symphony and 'In the
Steppes of Central Asia' in Western Europe, and fame began
to spread. Heart trouble and an attack of cholera under-
mined his health, and left little time for music.

1885. Visited Belgium and Paris, and met Liszt again at Weimar.

1886. Began a third symphony—never finished.

1887. Made further sketches for 'Prince Igor', but never finished
it. Had a heart attack at a fancy dress ball, and died
immediately.

Handsome, modest and kind. Trying to follow two professions probably contributed to his early death. Had no time to
write much music, and what he did write was frequently "improved" by well-meaning friends, such as Rimsky-Korsakov and
Glazounov, both before and after his death. They finished his
third symphony and 'Prince Igor', and changed many of his
completed works, usually to their detriment. Lyrical style,
combined with bold Russian colouring and harmonies.

Operas: 'Prince Igor' (left unfinished); 2 other operas (one
being unfinished); and an unfinished act for a ballet.

Three symphonies (third unfinished); tone poem, 'In the
Steppes of Central Asia'.

Chamber music, including 2 fine string quartets.

Fourteen songs, some to his own words.

A few piano pieces.

Biography and Chief Works of Peter Ilich Tschaikowsky

1840. Born in a small town in Central Russia, just west of the
Ural Mountains, where his father was a mining engineer.
But the family moved to St Petersburg (Leningrad) when he
was 10, and he was sent to the School of Jurisprudence. Had
music lessons, but showed no outstanding talent. (His name,
like those of most Russians, is spelled in various ways, because
there are no exact Roman equivalents to some of the letters in

the Russian alphabet. "Tchaikovsky" is gaining in popularity.)

1859. Appointed as clerk to Ministry of Justice. Music a hobby —improvised waltzes and polkas.

1861. Began to have serious music lessons and to consider becoming a musician. Went to St Petersburg Conservatoire, which was started in 1862 by Anton Rubinstein, a Russian pianist with a Germanic training and outlook.

1863. Gave up his post as civil servant, in order to devote himself to music, though at first he earned very little by it. Continued to study at the Conservatoire.

1866. Asked to teach harmony at newly formed Moscow Conservatoire, run by Anton Rubinstein's brother, Nicholas. They lived together. Compositions performed at Russian Musical Society. Wrote his first symphony. Visited sister in the country whenever he could. Shy and retiring, and loved the country.

1868. Met "the five". They prided themselves on their Russian characteristics, took Glinka as their model, and did not approve of Tschaikowsky's Germanic conservatoire training. His fantasy-overture 'Romeo and Juliet' was written under the influence of Balakirev, but "the five" and Tschaikowsky never really accepted each other. Tschaikowsky's music, having a closer link with European traditions, reached Western Europe before theirs did.

Fell in love with a Belgian opera singer, but she married someone else.

1874. Wrote piano concerto in B♭ minor, which soon became very popular in Europe and America.

1875. Ballet, 'Swan Lake'.

1876. Began to correspond almost daily with a wealthy widow, Mme von Meck, who loved his music, but did not wish to meet him, and never did so.

1877. Married, but separated after nine weeks. Fled to St Petersburg, then spent some weeks in Switzerland and Italy. Mme von Meck persuaded him to accept an annuity of about £600, so that he could be free of teaching (which he found very uncongenial), and live quietly in the country, giving all his attention to composition. Wrote his fourth symphony (the first famous one), and dedicated it to her. Also began his most famous opera, 'Eugene Onegin'. Made his home from

1877 to 1884 with his sister at Kamenka (the Kamenka period), though spent a good deal of time abroad.   Violin concerto in 1878.

1881. Offered position as Head of Moscow Conservatoire after death of Nicholas Rubinstein, but decided against it.   Wrote piano trio to Rubinstein's memory.

1885. Bought a house at Klin, in the country between Moscow and St Petersburg—always had a house in this neighbourhood for the rest of his life.   By now had received world recognition, and began to accept invitations to conduct his works throughout Europe.

1888. Fifth symphony and fantasy-overture 'Hamlet'.   Ballet 'The Sleeping Beauty'.

1889. German tour, including Hamburg, where he met Brahms, who heard his fifth symphony and liked it.   Also a second visit to London, where his music was always very popular.

1890. Opera 'The Queen of Spades' written and produced. Mme von Meck wrote saying she could no longer afford his pension.   She never wrote to him again, which wounded him very much.

1891. Death of beloved sister, in whose home he had so often stayed.   She and Mme von Meck had been the most important women in his life.   Concert tour of America—guest of honour at formal opening of Carnegie Hall, New York.   Returned to Russia, and wrote 'Nutcracker' ballet.   Arranged suite from it a year later.

1892–3. The 'Pathetic' symphony (the sixth and last).   Continued to tour, but always suffered from homesickness. Visited London again, and received honorary degree at Cambridge.

1893. Died of cholera.

A cultured, shy, retiring man, who disliked teaching, and preferred to live alone in the country, though he conducted his own works in many places with success towards the end of his life. But he was not afraid of showing his feelings in his music, which is often full of passionate melancholy.   Has Russian characteristics, though not enough to satisfy the Russian Nationalists of the period.   But it is also based on nineteenth-century European traditions (more than that of other Russians), and owed much to Germany and Italy.   He had the Italian love of sensuous melody.

His chief appeal lies in his melodies and his exciting orchestral colouring. His favourite composer was Mozart.

Six symphonies, the 4th in F minor, 5th in E minor, and 6th (the 'Pathetic') in B minor being the most often played.

Orchestral works on a programmatic basis, 'Romeo and Juliet' and 'Francesca da Rimini' being the best known. Other orchestral works, including 3 suites and the popular '1812' overture.

Concertos: 2 for piano, no. 1 in B♭ minor being the better known; 1 violin concerto; 'Variations on a Rococo Theme' for 'cello; and other slighter works.

Chamber music: 3 string quartets of uneven quality; piano trio 'To the Memory of a great Artist' (A. Rubinstein); and other works, including a string sextet.

Ballets: 'Swan Lake'; 'The Sleeping Beauty'; 'The Nutcracker'. (Orchestral suite arranged from the latter also very famous.)

Many operas, not very successful. 'Eugene Onegin' and 'The Queen of Spades' the best.

Many other works, including songs, a few of which are good; rather second-rate piano pieces; unimportant choral works, etc.

Biography and Chief Works of Antonin Dvořák

1841. Born near Prague (Czecho-Slovakia). Father an innkeeper and butcher. Played the violin in father's band, and sang in parish church. Learnt music from village schoolmaster.

1857. Sent to the Organ School at Prague, where heard and played works by Schumann and Wagner.

1859. Joined a concert band in Prague, and then the theatre orchestra, in which he stayed till 1871. Smetana soon became its conductor. Composed steadily, though individual qualities not yet evident.

1873. Early compositions becoming known. Began to teach composition. Happy marriage—had six children.

1875–6. Influenced by Smetana, became conscious of his Czech musical heritage. Compositions became simpler and began to show individual characteristics. Wrote several good chamber works, some using the "Dumka", a national dance. Czech songs. 'Stabat Mater'. Given a state grant, but compositions only known in his own country, and none published.

1877. Brahms saw his compositions, and helped to get some published. The two composers became friends.

1878. Wrote a series of Slavonic dances, and began to use more Czech dances, such as Polka and Furiant, in his chamber and symphonic works.

1884. First of several visits to England. Conducted 'Stabat Mater' and a symphony and other works. Great popular success. Wrote a new symphony for the London Philharmonic Society, and 'The Spectre's Bride' for Birmingham. Bought himself a house in Southern Bohemia.

1884–1890. Composed many works: a good deal of chamber music, including the 'Dumky' trio; the symphony in G (no. 4); the 3 concert overtures 'Amid Nature', 'Carnival', and 'Othello'; the Requiem; etc.

1890. Another series of visits to England, where he received an honorary degree at Cambridge, and gave the first performance of the Requiem in Birmingham. England's appreciation gave him courage to continue with his own kind of music, when pressure was being put on him to adopt Germanic styles and to live in Vienna. Also visited Russia and Germany, and was given various Czech honours.

1891. Became professor of composition at Prague Conservatoire, thus helping future Czech composers.

1892. Invited to New York to direct the Conservatoire of Music. Stayed for three years. Appreciated as teacher, conductor and composer. He hoped to develop an American school of composition. Wrote the 'New World' symphony, inspired by "Hiawatha", and containing melodies of Negro or Red Indian type. Also the 'Nigger' quartet, the 'cello concerto, and other works.

1895. Returned to Prague Conservatoire, and was made its Director in 1901. Wrote symphonic poems and operas, based on Czech legends.

1904. Died in Prague.

A simple peasant, with regular habits, such as that of going to bed early. Loved nature. Very "Slav-conscious", and created much Czech and Slavonic music. Did not use or imitate folk tunes, but wrote his music in the same style. One of the most tuneful of composers, who also had a good sense of orchestration. Used plenty of counter melodies, with a wide range of dynamics, and effective woodwind parts. But never attained a wholly integrated style, or the power of organic development possessed by Brahms. Followed on the classical composers, preferring Beethoven and Brahms to Wagner and Liszt. His best-known works are his chamber music and his symphonies.

Nine symphonies, of which the best known are the D minor, op. 70 (no. 2), the G major, op. 88 (no. 4), and the E minor, 'The New World' (no. 5). (The numbering is peculiar, and number 5 is the last.)

Violin concerto; 'cello concerto in B minor; and other concerted works less frequently played.

Three linked concert overtures: 'Amid Nature'; 'Carnival'; and 'Othello'.

Slavonic rhapsodies and dances, symphonic poems, and other similar works.

Much tuneful and attractive chamber music: 15 string quartets, including the 'Nigger' quartet; 3 string quintets; a string sextet; a popular piano quintet; 2 piano quartets; 3 piano trios, including the 'Dumky' trio; and others.

Choral works: 'Stabat Mater'; Requiem; 'The Spectre's Bride'; and others.

A number of operas, rarely performed outside Czecho-Slovakia.

A number of slighter works, for violin and piano (including the sonatina); piano solo (including the Humoreskes); piano duet (including the Slavonic dances); songs (including the 10 'Biblical Songs'), and 7 Gypsy Songs (no. 4 is 'Songs my Mother taught me'.)

Chapter Nineteen

The Twentieth Century

We are too close to the music written in the first half of the twentieth century to be able to judge it, and to decide which of it will live or will have an influence on the future. Its diversity is the chief thing that strikes us, for it takes many forms, and experiments of all kinds have been or are in the process of being made. But it all appears to have three things in common, particularly to those who take the music of the nineteenth century as a standard. It seems to be less tuneful, largely because the melody is in short figures instead of in the long regular-phrased tunes to which we are accustomed; it is not usually in easy-to-follow, clear-cut forms such as the sonata form of the Viennese composers, and this makes it harder to grasp; and it makes so much use of dissonance that many people find it unpleasantly harsh. But it must be remembered that the dissonances of one period tend to become the consonances of the next. Monteverdi's discords, which seemed so exciting to his contemporaries, seem quite mild to us today.

Although the following paragraphs attempt to classify the different trends, they are necessarily over-simplified and tentative. Also it is impossible, in a book of this size and type, to mention every composer who has been active in this century.

It will be noticed that British composers are mentioned more than they have been in the preceding chapters. After the great Tudor period, English music suffered a decline, and the one great composer between 1600 and 1900, Henry Purcell, died too young to have much effect on our musical history. But at the end of the nineteenth century *Parry* (1848–1918) and *Stanford* (1852–1924) headed a renaissance of British music. Parry was the professor of music at Oxford, and later became Principal of the Royal College of Music, London, to which institution he appointed the Irishman, Stanford, as a teacher of composition. *Holst* (1874–1934), *Vaughan Williams* and *John Ireland* (1879–) were all pupils of Stanford at the College, and their influence spread down to the next generation, for all three became professors at the College. *Rubbra* (1901–) was a pupil of Holst, and *Britten* of John Ireland.

Arnold Bax (1883–1953) studied at the Royal Academy of Music, but although an Englishman, he was affected by Celtic influences. *Elgar*, *Delius* (1862–1934) and *Walton* were largely self-taught as far as composition was concerned.

Parry and Stanford were steeped in the nineteenth-century Germanic traditions. Their pupils Holst and Vaughan Williams explored the music of England's past: folk music, Tudor music, and the music of Purcell. It looked as if they might found an English Nationalist school, but their recognition by the greater musical world made such nationalistic assertion unnecessary, and our younger composers have been accepted on their own merits. We can be as proud of the music produced by British composers today as of that written in the days of the first Queen Elizabeth.

The Impressionists

Impressionism began with a group of French painters, among whom were Manet, Monet, Renoir, and Cézanne. They aimed at painting what could be seen at a quick glance, without recording every detail in the way that earlier painters had done. Some wonderful experiments in colour and atmosphere resulted. Although the movement started as early as 1859, it really became established with an impressionist exhibition in 1874.

The movement spread to French poets such as Mallarmé and Verlaine, who called themselves Symbolists, and who tried to evoke and suggest rather than to make direct statements. *Debussy* met Mallarmé in 1887, and from then onwards began to be associated with the impressionists and

symbolists, and to imbibe their ideas.   He applied them to
music in a most original way, and became the first musical
impressionist.   His prelude 'L'Après Midi d'un Faune' is
based on the poem of that name by Mallarmé; and his
operatic setting of Maeterlinck's play 'Pelléas et Melisande'
is very impressionistic, as are all his piano pieces.

Although *Ravel* showed much more clarity than Debussy
and was more classical in outlook, he too can be called an
impressionist.   So also can the British composers *Delius,
Bax, John Ireland,* and even, to a certain extent, *Vaughan
Williams.*   The Italian *Respighi* (1879–1936) and the
Spaniard *De Falla* (1876–1946) were impressionist composers,
too.

The Neo-Romantics

The neo-romantics, or late romantic composers, were
those who, while extending their idioms and resources in
various ways, built on the work of Wagner and Brahms, and
carried on nineteenth-century traditions.

Strauss owed much to Wagner in his operas and to Liszt
in his symphonic poems, though he is more of a realist than
either, and his harmonies are more astringent.   He writes
with mastery for a huge orchestra.

Sibelius was a highly original composer, with a vigorous,
rugged quality in his music that brings to mind the cold vast
countryside of Finland.   But his music is romantic, though
in a very masculine way, and he obviously has an affinity
with Brahms.   His 7 symphonies are some of the greatest
musical masterpieces of this century.

The Hungarian composer *Bartok* (1881–1945) was an
experimentalist who wrote in many different styles at
different periods of his life, though all of his music was
coloured by his Hungarian nationality, and his use of
Hungarian folk song.   But some of his works have a decided
romantic element in them.

Shostakovitch (1906–), the chief Russian composer of the
present generation, has a very varied style, partly because
he has to compose music as the Soviet authorities dictate,

and this obviously conflicts with his own natural tendencies. But much of his music is very romantic. He has written 11 symphonies.

In England *Elgar* was a warm romanticist, who owed much to Brahms and Franck, and who carried their traditions over into the twentieth century. So also did *Vaughan Williams*, though his music owes much to English Tudor and folk music, as well as to the nineteenth-century European composers. His friend and contemporary, *Gustav Holst*, who died in 1934, was fundamentally a neo-romantic, though he wrote in many styles, and was fond of complicated rhythms. *Walton*, after an anti-romantic phase in his youth, settled down in his middle age to writing romantic music with its roots in the past, though in a twentieth-century idiom. *Rubbra's* symphonies also have become progressively more romantic. Although *Vaughan Williams* occasionally wrote modal music, most of the music of these English composers is based on major and minor scale relationships, unlike that of some of the composers who are mentioned later.

The Anti-Romanticists

But there has also been a strong reaction against romanticism in the twentieth century. *Stravinsky* (1882–) led the way. A Russian, and a pupil and friend of Rimsky-Korsakov, his first triumphs were in Paris, where he was invited by the great master of ballet, Diaghilev, to write music for his new kind of ballet, in which music, dancing and décor were equally important. 'The Fire Bird', 'Petrouchka' and 'The Rite of Spring' followed each other, each more original, more anti-romantic, more cacophonous than the last. 'The Rite of Spring', produced in 1913, caused an uproar in the theatre; and even today its astringent harmonies and contrapuntal clashes, and its primitive, yet complex, rhythms repel many people. But it placed him as the leader of a new style of music, and he had many imitators.

After this, Stravinsky began to write for smaller, though often unusual, combinations, and he adopted a severe, anti-emotional style: abstract, formal and impersonal. He became a "neo-classicist", taking the abstractions of eighteenth-century music as his model. This style, too, had its followers, composers who were going "back to Bach", though it left the general public bewildered and hostile. His 'Symphonies of Wind Instruments', his 'Concerto for Piano and Wind', and his 'Symphony of Psalms', which uses voices, but no violins, violas or clarinets, belong to this period.

Stravinsky settled in America in 1940, and his work took on a new vitality. He wrote two symphonies; and his opera 'The Rake's Progress' dates from 1951. But his music still continues to be controversial, and it arouses emotions in the hearer similar to those produced by Picasso in art.

The German, *Hindemith* (1895–) is another anti-romanticist and neo-classicist, who delights in line drawing rather than in harmony, and in letting the lines clash. He, too, settled in America. He is a violist, and his viola concerto is one of his best-known works. But he has written concertos for a number of instruments, as well as an opera, several symphonies and much chamber music.

The music of the Frenchman, *Honegger* (1892–1955) is rather similar. His concert opera 'King David', and his 'Pacific 231', an orchestral description of a steam engine, are two of his best-known works.

Bartok (1881–1945) went through a neo-classical phase, and *Prokofiev* delighted in writing rhythmically exhilarating, unromantic music, until ordered by the Soviet authorities to write in a more popular, lyrical style. In England *Walton* went through a similar phase in youth, but developed a warmer, more romantic style in later life. *Goossens* (1893–) is another anti-romantic and neo-classical English composer.

Experiments with Scales, Intervals, and Key

From the early seventeenth century until the end of the nineteenth, all Western European music has been based on tonality. That is to say, it has been written in a major or minor key, with chords based on the key, and modulations related to the main key centre. The chords have progressively become more discordant and chromatic, and the modulations have ranged further and further away from the key centre; but always there *has* been a key centre, to which everything has been related.

Wagner stretched the principles of tonality to the utmost, both with regard to chords and key relationships. So it was natural that twentieth-century composers should feel that they could go no further along that road, and should look for some new method of expressing themselves.

Debussy began to make use of the whole tone scale (C D E F♯ G♯ A♯ C). If you play this scale, or chords based on it, you will realise that it produces a very vague effect. You lose the sense of tonality, because, when every interval is the same size, every note appears to be equally important. There is, for example, no leading note rising a semitone to a tonic to help to produce a cadence. And as only two scales exist (on C and C♯), variety caused by modulation or key contrast is very limited. Even Debussy only used the scale occasionally, and it has been used very little since.

Other composers reverted to the ecclesiastical modes used by the sixteenth-century composers. *Vaughan Williams* often made deliberate use of these; and his writing was much affected by Tudor music, as, for example, in his 'Fantasia on a Theme of Tallis'. He even, occasionally, used an older style still, as in his G minor Mass, where he has much movement in parallel fourths and fifths, rather like the medieval organum. *Bartok*, the Hungarian composer, also wrote much modal music, based on his researches in Hungarian folk melody.

There was also an attempt to make use of scales with more than twelve notes to the octave. The Czech, *Alois Haba* (1893–), has written music based on scales of quarter tones and even sixth tones, though he has had few imitators. To Western ears it merely sounds out of tune. Also it is difficult to sing, and, except in the case of string instruments, it requires specially made instruments for its performance, so it is unlikely to have much future.   It is sometimes called "microtonal" music.

Other composers have made an attempt to build chords other than on the usual classical system of thirds.   The Russian *Scriabin* (1872–1915) tried building chords of various sizes of fourths, taken from an artificially manufactured scale; and *Schönberg* (1874–1951), at one stage, tried something similar, notably in his first chamber symphony.

Another form of experiment has been to write in two or more keys at once (bi-tonality or poly-tonality).   This has been tried by a number of composers, including *Strauss*, *Ravel*, *Milhaud* (1892–), *Honegger* and *Stravinsky*.   But the ear finds it difficult to assimilate more than one key at a time, and either one key gains the ascendancy, or the impression is given of no key at all (atonality).   There are occasions, however, when bi-tonality can give a very piquant effect.

Hindemith has invented a novel system of arbitrary relationships based on the complete chromatic scale.   He still believes in a tonal centre, but the application of his artificial system has produced some very unusual effects.

But perhaps the most talked-of innovation in this century has been that of the Austrian composer *Schönberg's* use of tone rows, and his complete rejection of all forms of tonality. He began by using the language of Wagner, though he thought in counterpoint rather than in harmony.   The cantata, the 'Gurrelieder', dates from this time.   But soon he set out to overthrow the key centre, and to write atonal music, in which all the twelve sounds of the chromatic scale were equally important.   He rebelled against the harmonic idioms of the nineteenth century, and turned to Bach for his rhythm and counterpoint.   'Pierrot Lunaire' for speaking voice and five instrumentalists is an atonal work of this period.   By 1923 he had evolved a new technique called "serial composition" or "twelve note technique", in which he based each composition on a different series of notes, consisting of all the twelve sounds of the chromatic scale, taken not scale-wise but in some arbitrary order, which he called a "tone row" (i.e. a row of notes).   Gradually a whole new system was built on these tone rows. Having once been stated, the series could be transposed, inverted, or played backwards, or segments of it could be grouped into chords. The notes could appear in any rhythm, so that a kind of a tune resulted, but usually with such extraordinary intervals between one note and the next that the effect was completely atonal.

Schönberg wrote many works using this new technique, one of the best known being his extremely difficult violin concerto. They created much opposition, and in 1933 he was dismissed from his post in Berlin, to which town he had moved from his native Vienna. He eventually settled in America, where he died in 1951. He had many pupils, both in Europe and America, two of the best known being his compatriots, *Berg* (1885–1935) (who wrote the opera 'Wozzeck') and *Webern* (1883–1945). But although Schönberg's theories were given to the world as long ago as 1923, and although he has had many disciples, his ideas have not, so far, been generally accepted, even by musicians, and time alone will show whether they have a lasting effect on the course of music.

Finally, mention should perhaps be made of the German experiments in electrophonic music, and the French "musique concrète", both of which began about 1948. Neither of these are "music" as the term is generally understood. The former consists of sounds produced by electrophonic instruments, and the latter of natural sounds which are combined or deliberately distorted, and both are recorded on tape. They will obviously be useful as "background" effects for film, radio and television, but whether they will have a future as a new kind of "music", it is too early to say.

Biography and Chief Works of Claude Achille Debussy

1862. Born near Paris of an unmusical family, but showed musical talent at an early age.

1873. Sent to Paris Conservatoire.

1884. Won the Prix de Rome, for cantata 'L'Enfant prodigue'. This prize carries residence in Italy. While in Rome began to change his ideas. The compositions he sent back to France shocked the conservatoire.

1887. Returned to France, and set about acquiring literary culture. Attracted to poet Mallarmé, and to impressionist painters. Became one of their "set". Wrote several collections of songs. Had previously been under the influence of Wagner and Moussorgsky, and French composers older than himself. Now thought out new harmonic system.

1892. Wrote prelude 'L'Après Midi d'un Faune', based on a poem of Mallarmé's. Entirely new harmony, orchestration and rhythm. Equivalent of impressionistic painting. Use of whole-tone scale, and parallel discords.

1893. Wrote a string quartet, also on new lines, and a number of other works.

1902. Opera 'Pelléas et Mélisande', on the play by Maeterlinck. Suggestive and impressionistic, creating a dream-like, otherworldly atmosphere. Based on free recitative.

1908. Conducted concerts in London, and again in 1909. Also Vienna and Budapest in 1910. Later, became very ill, but continued to compose.

1918. Died.

An impressionist composer. Revolted against both classicism and romanticism. Occasional use of whole-tone scale. Addition of 2nds and 6ths to triads. Use of overtones and parallel discords. A new pianistic idiom, making much use of the pedal. Very individual style, not used by succeeding composers.

Opera: 'Pelléas et Melisande'.

Orchestral works: Prelude 'L'Après Midi d'un Faune'; 3 symphonic sketches, 'La Mer'; 3 nocturnes; etc.

Chamber music: string quartet; sonata for flute, viola and harp.

Piano: 2 Arabesques; 'Suite Bergamasque'; 'Children's Corner Suite'; 6 'Images', including 'Reflets dans l'Eau'; 24 preludes, including 'La Cathédrale engloutie'; etc.

Songs: set many poems by contemporary French poets, such as Verlaine's 'Ariettes oubliées'.

Biography and Chief Works of Maurice Ravel

1875. Born in S. France, near Atlantic coast and Spanish border. Soon moved to Paris.

1889. Entered Paris Conservatoire, where had composition lessons from Fauré, a famous organist and composer, who later became head of the conservatoire. Also influenced by Liszt and the Russians. But soon developed individual style.

1902. Unsuccessfully competed for Prix de Rome, and again in 1903 and 1905. This finally caused a public outcry, as he had already produced technically competent and mature works, such as 'Pavane pour une Infante défunte', 'Jeux d'Eau', and the string quartet.

Settled in Paris, as composer, living an uneventful life.

1903–1914. A period of song and piano composition: 'Sonatina', 'Gaspard de la Nuit', 'Valses Nobles et Sentimentales' for piano; 'Mother Goose' for piano duet; 'Shéhérazade' and 'Histoires Naturelles' for voice. Ravel conceived most of his works for piano, but often orchestrated them later, as, for example, 'Valses Nobles et Sentimentales' and 'Mother Goose' above. Also wrote opera 'L'Heure Espagnole' and ballet 'Daphnis and Chloe'.

1914–1930. Growing tendency towards abstraction and simplification. More interested in line, less in colour. 'Le Tombeau de Couperin' for piano; sonata for violin and 'cello; 'La Valse' and 'Bolero' for orchestra; opera 'L'enfant et les Sortilèges'; and the orchestration of Moussorgsky's 'Pictures from an Exhibition'.

1922. Conducted at Queen's Hall, London. Also visited Holland and Venice.

1928. Tour of U.S.A., and another visit to England.

1930–1931. Piano concerto for the left hand; piano concerto in G major.

1932. Involvement in car crash caused a nervous breakdown, from which he never recovered.

1937. Died, after an operation on the brain.

An impressionist, rooted in classicism. Music akin to that of Debussy, but firmer and clearer in outlines and harmony, more formal and classical. Very French, civilised and restrained.

Preferred to write on a small scale.   Wrote many of his works for piano at first, but later orchestrated them skilfully.

Piano music: 'Pavane pour une Infante défunte'; 'Jeux d'Eau'; 'Sonatina'; 'Gaspard de la Nuit'; 'Valses Nobles et Sentimentales'; 'Le Tombeau de Couperin'; etc.

A number of songs.

Orchestral arrangements of his own piano works, such as 'Pavane' and 'Le Tombeau de Couperin', and of Moussorgsky's 'Pictures from an Exhibition'.   The 'Bolero' is the only purely orchestral work originally conceived for orchestra, and consists of one long *crescendo* caused by the gradual addition of more instruments.   Two piano concertos, one being for left hand only.

Ballets: 'Daphnis and Chloe'; 'Mother Goose'; 'La Valse'.

Operas: 'L'Heure Espagnole'; 'L'Enfant et les Sortilèges'.

Chamber music: string quartet; Introduction and Allegro for harp, string quartet, flute and clarinet; sonata for violin and 'cello; etc.

Biography and Chief Works of Richard Strauss

1864. Born in Munich, Bavaria.   Son of a horn player.   Began to compose in classical style in early youth.

1882. Entered Munich University, but left a year later to devote himself to music.   Composed in style of Brahms.

1885. Assistant music director at Meiningen.   Became converted to style of Berlioz, Liszt and Wagner.

1886. Assistant conductor of Munich opera.   Published some songs, and violin sonata.

1889. Assistant conductor at Weimar.   Symphonic poem 'Don Juan' performed there.

1890. 'Death and the Transfiguration'.   Works causing controversy.

1894. Married Weimar opera singer.

1895. Appointed conductor of Philharmonic concerts in Berlin. 'Till Eulenspiegel's Merry Pranks'.   Began conducting tours all over Europe.

1897. 'Don Quixote'.   Conducted in London.

1898. 'Ein Heldenleben'.   Appointed conductor of Royal Opera House in Berlin.

1903. Strauss festival in London.

1905. Opera 'Salome' caused even more controversy.

1909. Operas 'Elektra' and 'Der Rosenkavalier'.

1912. Opera 'Ariadne auf Naxos'.

Continued to compose operas, choral and orchestral works, and songs, but his later works are performed much more rarely than his earlier ones. The second horn concerto and the oboe concerto are two of his best later works.

1949. Died in Garmisch, Bavaria.

Early symphonic poems caused great controversy, but have now been accepted into the repertoire. Strauss refused to recognise a distinction between abstract and programme music. He believed that all good music is expressive: it can express states of mind and arouse similar emotions in the hearer. He used a very large orchestra and was a master of orchestration, using solo instruments most felicitously to represent people and characteristics.

His operas are extraordinarily varied. 'Salome' and 'Elektra' express the extremes of passionate excitement, while 'Der Rosenkavalier' is a Viennese musical comedy with a Mozartian turn of melody. But all show great powers of characterisation, and make use of *Leitmotiv*.

Symphonic poems: 'Don Juan'; 'Death and the Transfiguration'; 'Till Eulenspiegel's Merry Pranks'; 'Thus spake Zarathustra'; 'Don Quixote'; 'Ein Heldenleben'; etc.

Concertos: 2 for horn; 1 for oboe; 1 for violin.

Sonata for violin and piano, and other chamber works.

A large number of German *Lieder*, all of which are very expressive, and some, such as 'Morning' and 'Serenade' very beautiful.

15 operas, including 'Salome'; 'Elektra'; 'Der Rosenkavalier'; 'Ariadne auf Naxos'.

Biography and Chief Works of Jean Sibelius

1865. Born in Finland, son of a doctor. Started to learn the piano at 9, and the violin at 15.

1884. Entered Helsingfors (now Helsinki) University to study law, but allowed to have music lessons at the Conservatoire as well.

1885. Decided to become a composer.

1889. Won a Finnish state scholarship to Berlin, and later went on to Vienna, where he studied with disciples of Brahms.

1893. Returned to Finland, where he taught violin and composition at Helsingfors Conservatoire, and began to compose works based on Finnish legends, of which 'En Saga' and 'The Swan of Tuonela' are now the best known.

1897. Given a life grant by state, and thus enabled to devote himself entirely to composition.

1899. The tone poem 'Finlandia' aroused such patriotic demonstrations that it was banned by the Russian government which then ruled Finland.

1905. Conducted his second symphony in Berlin.

1912. Conducted his fourth symphony in Birmingham.

1914. Visited the U.S.A. and taught for a time in Boston. Given an honorary degree at Yale.

1918. Fighting in Finland, as the result of the Russian revolution, made him a temporary prisoner, but he continued to compose.

1921. Conducted fifth symphony in London.

But still not recognised as a great composer outside Finland, and spent most of his time living quietly in his Finnish home with his wife and daughters.   His music was not revolutionary enough to attract attention, as did that of Debussy or Stravinsky, and its bleak severity prevented easy understanding and appreciation.

1923. Sixth symphony, followed by seventh a year later.

1925. Symphonic poem, 'Tapiola'.   Creative activity began to wane; but his works were now achieving recognition in England and America, and, as time went on, in other countries too. Continued to live quietly.

1957. Died in Finland.

The first great Finnish composer, very conscious of his national heritage, and much revered in Finland.   Great love of nature, particularly as it is seen in the cold, vast stretches of Finland. Famous chiefly for his symphonies and his Finnish national tone poems.

Seven symphonies, all important works, but very different from each other.

Symphonic tone poems and suites based on Finnish legends, such as 'En Saga'; 'Karelia'; 'The Swan of Tuonela'; 'Finlandia'; and 'Tapiola'.

Violin concerto and a few other slighter works for violin and orchestra, or violin and piano.

Incidental music, choral works, a string quartet, piano pieces and songs.

Biography and Chief Works of Serge Prokofiev

1891. Born in Russia. A musical prodigy. Entered St Petersburg (Leningrad) Conservatoire, and studied under Rimsky-Korsakov and others. A brilliant pianist as well as composer.

1914. Left conservatoire. Continued to compose, completing his 'Classical' symphony in 1917. Had written 3 piano concertos, a violin concerto and 4 piano sonatas by this date.

1918. Travelled to London, Paris and Japan. Then settled in U.S.A.

1921. Opera 'The Love of Three Oranges' produced in Chicago.

1922. Moved to Paris, where his first violin concerto was produced in 1923.

1927. Returned to Russia, though made frequent visits to Western Europe, particularly when newly composed symphonies or concertos were performed. Later, the Soviet authorities prohibited travel, and ordered him (and other composers) to adopt a simpler, more lyrical style. He appeared to acquiesce, though some individuality still remains in his later works.

1936. Wrote 'Peter and the Wolf' for a children's concert in Moscow.

1953. Died in Moscow.

Began as a brilliant, precocious pianist and composer, writing original, fantastic yet unromantic, rhythmically exhilarating, and often discordant music. The early 'Classical' symphony exhibits these traits, in spite of its title. Later, at the Soviet command, he changed to a simpler, more lyrical style, though there are still traces of the earlier Prokofiev.

Six symphonies, including the 'Classical' (no. 1).

Five concertos for piano, 2 for violin and 1 for 'cello.

'Peter and the Wolf' for narrator and orchestra.

Seven operas, the best known being 'The Love of Three Oranges'.

Six ballets (some produced by Diaghilev).

A large number of brilliant piano pieces, some chamber music, and songs.

Biography and Chief Works of Edward Elgar

1857. Born near Worcester, son of Roman Catholic organist and owner of music shop, who played the violin in the Three Choirs Festival Orchestra. Grew up in provincial musical atmosphere. Played violin, bassoon, organ and piano.

1872. Entered a solicitor's office, but continued musical activities.

1879. Had a few violin lessons in London. Appointed band master of County Lunatic Asylum, member of Birmingham orchestra, and conductor of Worcester amateur orchestra. Composed small works.

1889. Married daughter of major-general, who proved to be a devoted wife, and bore him one daughter. Spent two years in London.

1891. Moved to Malvern, where he wrote a number of choral works, of which the best known are 'From the Bavarian Highlands', and 'Caractacus' (1898). All rather ordinary, and typical of choral works of the period.

1899. A great change suddenly came over his work with the appearance of his fine 'Enigma Variations'.

1900. 'The Dream of Gerontius' (poem by Cardinal Newman) performed with little success in Birmingham. Its new musical idiom and the Roman Catholic theology of its poem prevented its appreciation. But Jaeger ("Nimrod" of 'Enigma' variations), his friend at Novello's, got it performed at the Lower Rhine Festival, and then it became accepted in England, and gave a new standing to the composer.

1903. Started a trilogy of oratorios on the subject of the founding of the Christian church, but only wrote 'The Apostles' in 1903, and 'The Kingdom' in 1906. Also 'Pomp and Circumstance' marches, the concert overtures 'Cockaigne' and 'In the South'; and 'Introduction and Allegro' for strings.

1904. Moved to Hereford. Knighted. An Elgar festival held in London.

1905. Visited U.S.A., and made doctor of music at Yale University. (Had previously been given honorary degree of Oxford and Cambridge.) Professor of Music, Birmingham University, 1905–8.

1908. First symphony performed in Manchester and London.

Performed 100 times within a year. Now living in London. Violin concerto, second symphony, and symphonic study 'Falstaff' followed in the next few years.

1911. Given Order of Merit.

1914–1918. Produced a number of cantatas and other works connected with the war, which have not lived.

1919. Violin sonata, string quartet and piano quintet; 'cello concerto, slighter than his other orchestral works.

1920. Lady Elgar died. Retired to country. Composed nothing more of importance. (The slight 'Nursery Suite', composed for the future Queen Elizabeth II and her sister, belongs to this period.)

1934. Died in Worcester.

A late romantic composer who owed much to Berlioz, Mendelssohn and Wagner. He was not interested in English folk music, but his music is very English, in spite of this. Wrote sentimental, popular, and also bombastic, patriotic music, in addition to his great works. Normally used a large orchestra, and is, at times, very noisy.

Choral works: 'The Dream of Gerontius'; 'The Apostles'; 'The Kingdom', and many unimportant secular cantatas. Some popular part songs.

Orchestral works: the 'Enigma' variations; the concert overtures 'Cockaigne', and 'In the South'; 'Introduction and Allegro, for strings'; symphonic poem 'Falstaff'; 2 symphonies; violin concerto; 'cello concerto; and many other smaller works, of varying merit.

Chamber music: violin sonata; string quartet; piano quintet.

Biography and Chief Works of Ralph Vaughan Williams

1872. Born in Gloucestershire, son of a vicar. Educated at Charterhouse, Cambridge and Royal College of Music, London. Pupil of Parry and Stanford.

1896. Combined posts as organist and lecturer with travel and further study in Berlin, and, later, under Ravel in Paris. Developed slowly as a composer.

1901. Took Mus.D. at Cambridge. Began to take an interest in collecting English folk songs, and used their idioms in his own

songs.   Explored countryside, imbibing its atmosphere.   Wrote
3 Norfolk Rhapsodies, into which folk tunes were integrated.

1905. 'Towards the Unknown Region' for chorus and orchestra.
Began the 'Sea' symphony. (Words of both by Walt
Whitman.)

1909. 'On Wenlock Edge' for tenor, string quartet and piano,
and other works for vocal solo, chorus and orchestra.   Also
'Fantasia on a Theme by Tallis', and incidental music for
Aristophanes' 'Wasps', which was performed at Cambridge.

1911–1914. Wrote first opera, 'Hugh the Drover', and second
symphony, the 'London', partly programmatic.

1914–1918. Served in army throughout the war.

1919. Made teacher of composition at Royal College of Music.
Compositions began to get known both in England and
abroad, particularly at Contemporary Music Festivals.

1922. 'Pastoral' symphony (no. 3) produced, and Mass in G
minor written.

1924. 'Hugh the Drover' produced by Royal College of Music,
and then on professional stage (a rarity for any English opera
to be produced at that time).

1925. A series of sacred vocal works, such as 'Sancta Civitas',
'Benedicite'.

1931. 'Job', a masque for dancing.

1935. Fourth symphony, a harsh, stark work.   Received Order
of Merit.

1938. 'Serenade to Music' for 16 solo voices, written for Sir
Henry Wood's jubilee, and later arranged for solos, chorus and
orchestra.

1940. Began to write for films.   "Forty-ninth Parallel" was the
first.

1943. Fifth symphony.

1948. Sixth symphony.   Film music for "Scott of the Antarctic"
from which 'Sinfonia Antartica' (seventh symphony) was
produced in 1953.

1949. Opera 'The Pilgrim's Progress', produced in 1951 for
Festival of Britain.

1956. Eighth symphony.

1957. Ninth symphony.

1958. Died.

A truly English composer, who, after a late start, developed a style of his own, in which folk tunes, Tudor idioms, movement of parallel concords, a sacred and mystical element, a contemplative style and a love of the country are all blended. A prolific composer who wrote in many forms.

Orchestral works: 9 symphonies—all mentioned above; overture to the 'Wasps'; 'Fantasia on a Theme of Tallis'; 'Fantasia on Greensleeves', etc; 'The Lark Ascending' for violin and orchestra; oboe concerto; romance for harmonica, etc.

Choral works: 'Mass in G minor'; 'Sancta Civitas'; 'Benedicite'; and many others.

A number of hymns, including the tune 'Sine Nomine' to the words 'For all the Saints'.

Five operas, including 'Hugh the Drover', and 'The Pilgrim's Progress'. Ballets, including 'Job'.

Many songs, including 'Linden Lea'; 'Silent Noon'; 'Songs of Travel'; 'The Water Mill'. Also some fine part songs. 'Serenade to Music' for 16 solo voices.

Some chamber music.

Film music, including "Scott of the Antarctic".

Biography and Chief Works of William Walton

1902. Born in Oldham, Lancashire. Father a musician.

1912. Sent to Christ Church Choir School, Oxford, and had lessons from Sir Hugh Allen. Began to compose.

1918. Entered Oxford University. Wrote piano quartet, which was later published by Carnegie Trust. Became friendly with the Sitwells (a famous family of writers, two brothers and a sister). They encouraged him to leave Oxford, to live with them and to devote himself to composition. Travelled abroad with them also.

1922. Composed string quartet, which was performed at the Salzburg Contemporary Music Festival in 1923. Also wrote 'Façade', an "entertainment" for speaking voice and six instrumentalists, to Edith Sitwell's words. Contained parodies of jazz, popular songs and Rossini, as well as some beautiful numbers. Shocked audiences, who were not used to humour in concert music. Several revisions later, and more poems added. Later again turned into two suites for full orchestra, and also into ballets.

1925. Overture 'Portsmouth Point', first work for full orchestra. Gay and lively.

1927. 'Sinfonia Concertante' for piano and orchestra (revised in 1943).

1929. Viola concerto—begins with a slow movement. A fine, romantic and well-knit work.

1931. Oratorio 'Belshazzar's Feast'. Uses large orchestra, and is full of pagan colour.

1934. First symphony performed without the finale, which had not yet been written. Again begins with a slow movement. Began to write for films.

1937. 'Crown Imperial March', for coronation of George VI. Also 'In Honour of the City of London', for chorus and orchestra.

1939. Violin concerto, another romantic work, again beginning with a slow movement.

    During the war was commissioned to compose music for films. 'Spitfire' prelude and fugue, for film "The First of the Few", and music for the film of "Henry V" have lived outside their ephemeral medium.

1945. Toured Scandinavia, as conductor, for British Council.

1947. Quartet in A minor.

1948. Opera 'Troilus and Cressida', based on Chaucer's version of the story. Visited Argentina, and married an Argentinian.

1951. Knighted.

1953. 'Orb and Sceptre' march for coronation of Elizabeth II.

1957. 'Cello concerto. Johannesburg Festival Overture.

1958. Partita for orchestra.

A slow worker, with a relatively small output but a very high standard of workmanship. Early works tended to be discordant, but very alive rhythmically. A romantic vein appeared in his later work. Always virile. Not a devotee of any modern "ism". Shows a consistent development from the music of the past. Most of his music is tonal (based on major and minor scales), though using modern discords.

Orchestral works: 1 symphony; 'Sinfonia Concertante' for piano and orchestra; viola concerto; violin concerto; 'cello concerto; overtures 'Portsmouth Point', Scapino' and Johannesburg

Festival Overture; two 'Façade' suites; marches 'Crown Imperial' and 'Orb and Sceptre'.

Choral works: 'Belshazzar's Feast'; 'In Honour of the City of London'; 'Te Deum' for coronation of Elizabeth II; and a few others.

Opera: 'Troilus and Cressida'.

Chamber music: piano quartet; string quartet; violin sonata.

Film music, from which has been rescued 'Spitfire' prelude and fugue, from "The First of the Few"; and concert suite and two pieces for strings from "Henry V".

Biography and Chief Works of Benjamin Britten

1913. Born in Lowestoft, East Anglia. A prodigy. Studied piano and composition while at a public school.

1925. 'A Simple Symphony' for strings (revised in 1934.) Went on to Royal College of Music, London, where studied composition with John Ireland.

1933. Wrote a number of slight choral works. Gradually began to write music for films, incidental music for plays, etc.

1937. 'Variations on a Theme of Frank Bridge' for string orchestra, played at Salzburg Festival. Began to write the piano and the violin concertos.

1940. 'Seven Sonnets of Michelangelo' for voice and piano. Went to U.S.A.

1941. String quartet, followed by another in 1945.

1942. 'Hymn to St Cecilia', 'A Ceremony of Carols', and other choral works. Also song cycles for solo voice with orchestra or piano, including 'Serenade' and 'The Holy Sonnets of John Donne'. Also collections of folk songs.

1945. Having achieved a mastery of the setting of words, and having had dramatic experience through writing music for films and plays, was now ready to produce opera. 'Peter Grimes' was an immediate success, both in England and abroad. 'Four Sea Interludes' and 'Passacaglia' from it also performed separately as orchestral music.

Settled in Suffolk, where he started the small annual Aldeburgh Festival.

1946. 'The Young Person's Guide to the Orchestra' (also called 'Variations on a Theme of Purcell'). Chamber opera 'The Rape of Lucretia'.

1947. 'Albert Herring', a comic opera.

1949. 'Let's Make an Opera' a children's play containing a small opera 'The Little Sweep'. 'Spring' symphony, for chorus and orchestra.

1951. Opera 'Billy Budd', with all-male cast.

1953. Opera 'Gloriana' written for coronation of Elizabeth II.

1955. Opera 'The Turn of the Screw'.

1957. Ballet 'Prince of Pagodas'.

1958. 'Noye's Fludde', a children's opera.

A prolific, clever and imaginative composer, whose greatest strength seems to lie in his setting of words, either in songs, choral works or operas. Has an affinity with Purcell. Is also an excellent pianist and accompanist.

Operas: 'Peter Grimes'; 'The Rape of Lucretia'; 'Albert Herring'; 'The Little Sweep' (contained in 'Let's Make an Opera'); 'Billy Budd'; 'Gloriana'; 'The Turn of the Screw'; 'Noye's Fludde'.

A large number of choral works, including 'Hymn to St Cecilia', 'A Ceremony of Carols'; 'A Spring Symphony'.

Songs, mostly in cycles, including 'Seven Songs of Michelangelo'; 'The Holy Sonnets of John Donne'; 'Les Illuminations'; 'Serenade for tenor, horn and strings'; and arrangements of folk songs.

Orchestral works: 'A Simple Symphony'; 'Variations on a Theme of Frank Bridge'; 'Variations and Fugue on a Theme of Purcell'; and others. Piano concerto; violin concerto.

Chamber music: 2 string quartets, and a few other works.

Music for films and incidental music.

INDEX

Page numbers in **black print** are the more important references. (A large number of musical works are listed in the biographies, chapters fourteen to nineteen, that are not referred to in this index.)